Contents

Foreword

The Twenty-first Annual Course and Conference of the United Kingdom Reading Association was held at Dundee College of Education, from 23 to 27 July 1984.

The theme for the Conference, 'Reading and the New Technologies', was, in one sense, a much narrower and more prescriptive theme than for many of the preceding conferences. It may have been seen as 'taking a chance' to plan for such a Conference, particularly in view of the need to decide upon the Conference theme so many months in advance of it taking place.

It appears, however, that these earlier decisions were not far wrong and I believe that the selection of this theme was timely. Although very much more is undoubtedly happening than was mentioned at this Conference, it might be fair to claim that the papers presented and the workshops held give a reasonable view of the field at that time.

As is always the case, the papers in this volume are only a selection of those arising from the Conference. It has unfortunately been impossible to include them all, however worthy and informed they may be. I have arranged this volume into three parts in an attempt to identify the major concerns, the relevant issues and examples of current and developing practice. The papers in all three sections are important, but it is up to the reader to combine them in a way to meet his or her own needs.

I hope that the publication of the papers in this volume will lead to a wider and further examination of this important area of education.

Jim Ewing
President 1983–4

Reading ___ gies

Proceedings of the Twenty-first Annual Course and Conference
of the United Kingdom Reading Association,
Dundee College of Education, 1984

Edited by

HEINEMANN EDUCATIONAL BOOKS

Heinemann Educational Books Ltd
22 Bedford Square, London WC1B 3HH

LONDON   EDINBURGH   MELBOURNE   AUCKLAND
HONG KONG   SINGAPORE   KUALA LUMPUR   NEW DELHI
IBADAN   NAIROBI   JOHANNESBURG
PORTSMOUTH (NH)   KINGSTON   PORT OF SPAIN

British Library Cataloguing in Publication Data

United Kingdom Reading Association, *Conference*
  (21st: 1984: Dundee College of Education)
  Reading and the new technologies: proceedings
  of the twenty-first annual course and conference
  of the United Kingdom Reading Association,
  Dundee College of Education, 1984.
  1. Reading—Great Britain
  I. Title   II. Ewing, . ᵔ
  428.4′07′1041   LB1C

  ISBN 0-435-10909-X

Phototypesetting by Georgia Ltd, Liverpool
Printed and bound in Great Britain by
Biddles Ltd, Guildford and King's Lynn

Introduction

Reading and the new technologies

J. M. Ewing

When I first proposed the title 'Reading and the New Technologies' for this Conference, some two years ago, I had only a vague notion of what I meant. I recollect thinking that the new technologies were probably primarily based in microelectronics, though I did have some concern for some of our not-so-new technologies, particularly if they could be promoted and used in 'new' ways. I also clearly recall supporting the proposed Conference theme by suggesting that, by the summer of 1984, there would be sufficient happening in this area to support a major Conference. I thought then, as I feel today, that the United Kingdom Reading Association, being the prime professional association concerned with reading at all levels, should be the body to run such a Conference.

During the intervening period of two years, I have attempted to clarify my views about this Conference both in terms of how 'new' the technologies had to be for inclusion in the presentations and how much of a debate to encourage about the place of the new technologies in the development and teaching of reading. Although I have not lost my sympathy for the longer established technologies such as the overhead projector and the audio tape or cassette recorder, I feel I have been caught up in the rapidly moving tide of new developments, at least in terms of arranging the programme for this Conference. Of the presentations extolling the use and potential of the new technologies, you will find that virtually all will refer to microchip technology at one stage or another. Having been prepared to consider papers concerning the less advanced technology, such as the overhead projector, I found that I seldom had the choice. The very greatest majority of presenters are clearly in touch with the microprocessor.

This being so, I have tried to keep myself informed on current and future trends as they influence reading.

The pace of change

Within the world of microcomputers we are now accustomed to using superlatives, such as 'the greatest revolution of all time', 'the most rapidly growing industry', 'the smallest electronic circuitry' and 'the most economical way of storing and transmitting information'. Indeed, some of us will still be bemused at what is referred to as the fifth generation of computers, not having fully gathered what the preceding four generations were or indeed how one generation begets the next. Maddison (1982) describes the first-generation computer as being based on valves, the second generation on transistors and the third generation on the silicon chip. As far as I can gather, the fourth generation of computers takes the art of including more and more on to a single microchip, whereas the fifth generation is what Harley and Silcock (1984) call 'more than just a great leap forward – it is a leap in the dark'. This latest breed of computer will be able not only to acquire information but to use it intelligently too. Within the literature there are a number of texts (Rushby, 1981; Lewis and Tagg, 1980; Smith, 1982) which summarise the progress of computers in education in the United Kingdom, America and in many European countries. But it is perhaps only since 1979, with the advent of the microcomputer, that education has really noticed computers. Earlier work in places such as the Chelsea College of London University, the College of St Mark and St John, Plymouth and the London Borough of Havering did much to spearhead the more recent developments. Many of these projects and schemes have been graced with contrived yet attractive acronyms, some examples being C.A.M.O.L., C.I.C.E.R.O., P.L.A.T.O. and P.R.I.N.C.E.S.S. Clearly the exploratory work of these projects, all running during the 1970s, has done much to benefit subsequent developments which are happily now more widely applied across the nation. As Rushby (1981) suggests, one of the outcomes of the U.K. National Development Programme in Computer Assisted Learning was that it recruited relatively junior staff who became 'academic guerrillas trained in the politics of innovation and committed to computer based learning'. They have done much to foster the new initiatives now being shown in, for example, the two U.K. government programmes currently running, the Microelectronics Education Programme (D.E.S., 1981) and the Scottish Microelectronics Development Programme (S.M.D.P., 1981). Each of these programmes supports the government-backed plans to ensure that every school in the United Kingdom has and can use a microcomputer.

The pace of change is also reflected in both academic and popular literature. Up until about two years ago it was very rare to see an article in the mainstream academic journals relating to the influence or use of microcomputers in the field of education, much less relating to reading. One has only to glance at current issues to see that interests have clearly changed.

Today there is a different picture. The shelves of the bookstores and newsagents abound with popular magazines for the home computer enthusiast. The same happens in public libraries where the up-to-a-dozen computer magazines are more popular than *The Listener* or *Radio Times*. The libraries in academic institutions have seen an increase in education technology oriented learned journals, and there is even now a slow trickle of such articles beginning to appear in journals such as *Educational Research* and the *British Journal of Educational Psychology*.

Much of this press is devoted to the new ideas and applications of microchip technology with a significant proportion focusing on the ethical and management issues. For example, O'Donnell (1982) quotes Seymour Papert thus: 'During the 1980s small but immensely powerful computers will become as much part of everyone's life as the TV, the telephone, the printed page and the notebook. Indeed computers will integrate and supersede the functions of these and other communicational and recreational home technologies. I emphasize; this will happen independently of any decisions by the education community.' This view is repeated many times over, with frequent calls for reform in education or in government policy. Then we read Chandler (1984) on the Dynabook: 'a prototype personal computer the size of a pocket note-book allowing the user to save, retrieve and manipulate the content of its vast store of words, pictures and animations using a powerful language called 'Smalltalk'. To see how all this relates to the development and teaching of reading, I examined the literature further.

Recent specific developments

I find the changes almost overwhelming. As one might expect, computer technology is being applied to the calculating of readability levels for drill and practice and for information retrieval. In the drill and practice area there are now many programs which test language skills such as spelling, word meanings and punctuation. However restricted such programs may be, this use of the microcomputer has its refinements as described by Walton (1984). He prefers the term 'structured reinforcement' to 'drill and practice' and is at pains to suggest that, to be useful, such pupil activities must be interactive and placed in a meaningful context.

There are also many examples of information handling by the computer, and I do not cease to be amazed at the number of people who want to transfer maps to computer programs. We have world maps, country maps, city maps, street maps, railway maps, even maps showing the number of washer women in 1871.

Some of the more interesting innovations have been in the area of games and simulations. There are many examples of classical interaction games such as 'hide and seek' or 'hunt the thimble', and there are more sophisticated adventure games. Examples of simulations are also now appearing in schools and one of the most topical must be 'Mary Rose', which is a simulation of the recovery of treasure from King Henry VIII's flagship which sank in the Solent in 1545 and was recently raised. The pupil involvement in programs like this one and others are now well described in several texts (Obrist, 1983; Chandler, 1984; Garland, 1982).

Word processing in the teaching of reading and writing appears to be a little slower in its impact in schools. Of course to get the best from word processing packages, it is necessary to have a printer and, preferably, a disk drive. The building in of dictionaries and thesauruses to check spellings and suggest alternatives greatly enhances a child's progress with his or her own creative writing. Hardware developments of touch-sensitive keyboard and light pens enable the very young child and the physically handicapped to avail them-selves of the full facilities of word processors. More recently the Micro Writer and the Omni Reader have expanded yet further the possibilities of young children in mastering the challenges of reading and writing.

I cannot avoid a mention of Logo, a computing language originally developed by Papert and now widely used in artificial intelligence. Much of the work with school children was in fact carried out in the Department of Artificial Intelligence at Edinburgh University. Some of the outcomes of this will be familiar, in the Turtle, Bigtrak and the B.B.C. Buggy. The screen equivalents of these are also available. The universally acclaimed benefits of work with Logo are now widely known. The philosophy behind the development of Logo is described in Papert's best selling book *Mindstorms* (Papert, 1980). The programming language allows the child, learning by doing, to discover not only the result but also the means by which the result is achieved.

I also became aware of the changes in the field of telesoftware. It was valuable for me to learn the difference between teletext and viewdata. Teletext systems (the two examples in the U.K. are the B.B.C. CEEFAX and the I.T.V. ORACLE) are where information is broadcast and can be read on a suitably adapted television screen. Viewdata systems are where computer stored information is fed along a telephone line. The British public viewdata system is known as PRESTEL, and holds information from in excess of 500 different bodies ranging from the Aberdeen Harbour Board to the Zimbabwe Tourist Authority. Unlike teletext, the viewdata user has two-way communication with the information bank

More recently there has been videotex where it is now possible to load programs off air onto home or school computers. There is currently work going on based in the Brighton area to experiment with the transmission of computer software into schools; seven schools in England and two in Scotland are so far involved.

I am pleased to say that many of these aspects of the new technologies are dealt with very much more fully during the course of the Conference. You will meet a new species of the Turtle, the Tasmanian Turtle, with Val Walsh and you will learn more about the potential of word processors from David Wray and Carla Broderick. Speech synthesis will be examined by Reg Eyre and there will be many others examining the different approaches to programming: drill and practice, adventure games and simulation.

What happens next?

I am tempted to return to Papert's statement about the inevitability of computers superseding our more conventional technologies such as chalk and the printing press. I feel, perhaps like many of you will, that there can be no such inevitability. We are more in control of our fate, our educational fate at any rate, than Papert would seem to suggest.

I accept the inevitability of an improved technology, the way in which digitised speech may replace synthesised speech, the way in which glass fibres will replace copper wires, the way in which we will go further and faster and make things smaller. But I cannot accept that these changes will 'happen independently of any decision by the education community'.

I am also puzzled by the apparent divide between hardware and software.

4

We learn almost daily of the advances in the technology, the hardware, but of the limitations of the appropriate software to use it to the best advantage. We learn of the potential of network systems such as Micronet but of the paucity of usable material to employ such systems in schools fully. We hear of improving memory systems making it easier and easier for each child in a classroom to have his or her own personal computer memory. But what will such a memory contain? We hear of plans to store the entire contents of the *Oxford English Dictionary* on computer disk and of plans to link computer-held data with moving video pictures.

All of this, in a sense, is independent of educational decision making. But, I ask, need it be? Education must be the most expensive investment any nation has and, laying aside any political arguments, may be the investment to which many nations pay lip service.

I am not a de-schooler. I do not fully subscribe to the views of some, such as Professor Tom Stonier, that more education will take place in the home in the year 2000 than in the school. Obrist (1983) reports that around two million personal computers have been sold in Britain. We are also told that there are more home computers per head in the U.K. than in any other nation in the world. Obrist goes on to say that, with the use being made of the sophisticated technology already available, the home could become an important adjunct to education. He suggests that the signs are already with us that the educational computer programs used in school will arrive in the home. The future, he suggests, is that children will bring into school their own personal micros in the same way as they now bring their calculators, but micros complete with each child's own store of information and programs.

Chandler (1984) paints a rather more stark picture in suggesting that schools will not last for much longer unless they become far more responsive to change and more open to radical restructuring. He warns of the danger of going too far in transferring the information contained in books and newspapers to the electronic media. In 1984, he cautions against the destruction of permanent printed records and their replacement by computer controlled flexible records as graphically described by George Orwell (1949). In Orwell's 1984, the Ministry of Truth regularly 'updates' history according to the whim of the ruling party, with the discarding of inconvenient facts.

Of course, I say, it will never happen. But am I justified in using such a categoric word as 'never'? Chandler reports a suggestion made by Ronald Meighan of Birmingham University's Faculty of Education. Education, Meighan suggests, may move towards 'contracts' between parents and school based on children spending part of their learning time at home. 'In quite a short period of time the majority of homes are likely to be equipped as sophisticated information retrieval centres, whilst schools, starved of the necessary funds, will do no more than replace old text books.'

Hammond (1983) also describes some disturbing scenarios. He instances giant, unlit, unheated factories in Japan where armies of robots, working unassisted, 24 hours a day, 365 days a year, tirelessly manufacture and assemble more robots. I understand that even the union subscriptions for 200 robots are paid by a Japanese manufacturing company. Does this mean that machine intelligence has reached or is about to surpass human intelligence? I am inclined to call upon a higher deity than all of us to forbid it.

But let us be more positive. This Conference has been arranged to examine and debate reading and the new technologies. I think you will find every one of the sessions, papers and workshops are 'on target' with this theme. The focus of our deliberation therefore is firmly seated in the reading and language area. I would be surprised, however, if it remains there during some of the discussions. The wider issues are so vital that they must come to the surface on some occasions. Nor will you find, I trust, that every presentation promotes involvement in the new technologies to the same extent. Some, I expect, will counsel a 'stop and think about it' approach.

The study of reading is of prime interest to all of us at this Conference and we will all be concerned with enhancing our knowledge and our understanding of the place of the new technologies in reading. I do not expect there to be any major breakthrough for any delegate, whether it is in personal realisation or in technical achievement. I do expect, however, to see enthusiasm. I wish to remind you of a plea made by John Merritt (1983) two years ago at this Association's Conference. In speaking about reading in the twenty-first century, Merritt said: 'What we need now is not optimism but enthusiasm. Optimists despair when their own particular vision is not fulfilled. Enthusiasts keep going because they know that sooner or later we shall overcome each new educational problem no matter how intractable it may seem from our own necessarily limited contemporary perspective.'

In my planning of this Conference I had a vague notion that it might highlight the need for some co-ordination of the development of reading and the new technologies. I had a vision of the Conference expressing a need for planned development and research in this area. I further thought that the United Kingdom Reading Association was the most appropriate body to co-ordinate and manage such an exercise. I do not now think this will emerge but I am not disheartened. If all those present this week can say, twelve months from now, that partly as a result of attending this Conference they have advanced their own thinking and action, in whatever way is appropriate to each individual, then we will have made progress.

References

CHANDLER, D. (1984) *Young Learners and the Microcomputer*. Milton Keynes: Open University.

D.E.S. (1981) *The Microelectronics Education Programme: The Strategy*. London: Department of Education and Science.

GARLAND, R. (1982) *Microcomputers and Children in Primary School*. London: Falmer.

HAMMOND, R. (1983) *Computers and Your Child*. London: Century.

HARLEY, J. and SILCOCK, B. (1984) 'The Battle for the Fifth Generation', *The Sunday Times*, 1 July.

LEWIS, R. and TAGG, E. D. (1980) *Computer Assisted Learning*. London: Heinemann.

MADDISON, A. (1982) *Microcomputers in the Classroom*. London: Hodder & Stoughton.

MERRITT, J. (1983) 'Reading 2001: Where do we go from here?', in B. Gillham (ed) *Reading through the Curriculum*. London: Heinemann.

OBRIST, A. J. (1983) *The Microcomputer and the Primary School*. London: Hodder & Stoughton.

O'DONNELL, H. (1982) 'Computer literacy, part I: An overview'. *The Reading Teacher*, 35, pp. 490–94.

ORWELL, G. (1949) *Nineteen Eighty-Four*. London: Secker & Warburg.

PAPERT, S. (1980) *Mindstorms: Children, Computers and Powerful Ideas*. Brighton: Harvester.

RUSHBY, N. (1981) *Selected Readings in Computer-Based Learning*. London: Kogan Page.

S.M.D.P. (1981) *Strategy and Implementation Paper*. Glasgow: Scottish Microelectronics Development Programme.

SMITH, I. C. H. (1982) *Microcomputers in Education*. Chichester: Ellis Horwood.

WALTON, D. (1984) 'Structured reinforcement', in R. Jones (ed) *Micros in the Primary Classroom*. London: Edward Arnold.

Part I: Concerns

1 Reading and technology: tangibles and intangibles

Christian Gerhard

The *and* of the title should be replaced by a symbol such as ⊙ to convey the degree of interaction between these two areas. The relationship is extremely complex and this paper can only attempt to introduce a few points of special relevance to those who feel responsible for aspects of contemporary education. The history of the relationship alone could fill volumes. Space here prohibits any detailed account. A highly selective list of interesting events and suggested reading is provided at the end of the paper, all of it limited to our Western tradition.

The paper will attempt to introduce five main points.

1. Technological innovations as they affect reading are essentially extensions of the sensory and kinesthetic abilities of human beings. By tracing the stages of technological developments, we can better understand in what way they are related to people and their ways of thinking.

2. Reading during any historical period reflects a society's goals and values and therefore a particular use of language. Even technological innovations affecting reading occur, or are successful, as they relate to current goals and values.

3. Formal education is an important part of the political and economic structure of a society, giving access to power, and affected by technological change. The teaching of reading and particular use of language is at the heart of any formal education.

4. Those who teach reading need a broad general education in order to understand: (a) the goals and values of their society, (b) the technological changes that are taking place leading to changes in ways of thinking, (c) the role of language in the larger culture and its subcultures, and (d) the previous experience to which students have been exposed.

5. Largely because of technological changes taking place from one generation to the next, teachers have had a different set of experiences from their students. Nevertheless, they need to be sufficiently flexible to understand their students' needs and aspirations and the way the world looks to them. This is because no learning can take place unless

new information is incorporated into old. The new information may require developing new kinds of perception, or expectation, but these must also be linked to previous modes.

Technological innovations as extensions of human capabilities

The first main point, that technological innovations are essentially extensions of sensory and kinaesthetic abilities of human beings, is especially important in establishing a human framework for the new technology. Nobody has described it better as it relates to changes in thinking than Jerome Bruner. In an article entitled 'Growth of Mind' (1965), he says, 'The evidence today is that the full evolution of intelligence came as a result of bipedalism and tool using (p.437).' Without the development of tools, the large human brain would not have compensated for physical vulnerability. Primitive extensions of the hands with stone tools fashioned by individuals evolved slowly into cultural transmission of tool making and tool mastery. Language became an important part of this transmission. Unlike individuals in ape societies, young humans spend most of their time with adults who instruct and guide them in survival and in the mores of the tribe. Gradually, as the tribe grows, there is more knowledge within the social group than can be mastered by one person and teaching of the young becomes a specialised activity divorced from the experiences and tasks of daily life.

Bruner wrote:

> This very extirpation makes learning become an act in itself, freed from the immediate ends of action, preparing the learner for the chain of reckoning remote from pay-off that is needed for the formulation of complex ideas. (1966, p.1009)

At the time Bruner wrote this, he had cross-cultural evidence that schooling itself made a profound difference in thinking processes. Since that time there has been much additional evidence, such as the work of Scribner and Cole (1981). The dialogue between teacher and student which originated as part of tool making and mastery instruction appears to be at least as telling as the process of learning to read and write itself. Language when written is used abstractly, 'freed from the immediate ends of actions', and requires direction in how to approach it. This is especially the case with the phonetic alphabet, as compared to others, for meaning is abstracted from sound and then translated into a symbolic, visual code. As Marshall McLuhan wrote in *The Gutenberg Galaxy* (1962), a new way of perceiving the world evolved from the shift in perceptual weight from ear to eye; from listening to reading. At the same time, the written word 'detribalised' people by creating private, individual thinking space for interaction with language.

The stages of development can be traced in capsule form. Illiterate human-kind might be said to have lived in a world vibrant with sound and shared experience, where thought and action were intimately related, time and space

9

varied with geography, the seasons, and the weather, and art was part of the magical explanation of cause and effect illustrated by means of sacred objects.

Literate humankind, on the other hand, has learned detached habits of observation based on analysis of data unrelated to direct action, regards time and space from a fixed point of view determined by instruments, and looks at pictures as representations rather than as objects with magical significance.

Electronic humankind will learn to live with systems of symbolic abstraction one remove further from daily life than literate humans. Languages with little connection to the mother tongue or to daily life will probably be learned (Ong, 1977), at least until fifth or sixth generation computers using natural language are common. Written communication will be via machines capable of computing and transmitting information in seconds which was formerly slaved over by skilled people for weeks. Detached habits of observation will be mostly achieved by remote control and will include many systems for classifying and encoding information about process and content, as well as about storage and retrieval. Decoding these systems will mean taking many constraints into account.

While literate human beings are dependent on technological developments such as a good light, a pair of spectacles, a printing press whose ancestor was the Roman wine press, paper and ink, electronic human beings will be dependent on reliable sources of power, a machine complete with technician to repair it, complex books of instructions, and the ability to manipulate the machine in a reasonably efficient manner. Mukerji, writing in *From Graven Images: Patterns of Modern Materialism* (1983), speaks of our Western societies classifying our material goods under the label *economy*, while it is our *culture* which is now built around our patterns of consumption. We are what we own.

All of these changes in symbols and technology are reflected in reading patterns and attitudes. Medieval and early Renaissance readers wished to share in the wisdom and comfort of the Bible. Before the printing of the Gutenberg Bible in 1456, manuscripts were objects of veneration in themselves and when the book was the Bible, it partook of some of the magic which writing tends to dispel. In some societies this still holds true, but a utilitarian approach is far more typical. Most text read today is consumable, not even reaching a library shelf, and concerns the needs of the day.

Reading reflects a society's goals and values

The undeniable truth that there has been a basic change in attitudes towards reading since the Middle Ages serves to introduce the second point of this paper: that reading during any historical period reflects a society's goals and values and therefore a particular use of language. At the time of the Latin Gutenberg Bible, 1456, the Renaissance was in full swing, Leonardo da Vinci was a young boy, perspective painting, empirical science and advances in mathematics were on their way, but most of the populace of Europe followed the dictates of the Church, out of conviction, inertia or fear. Life in the next world was very close, with life expectancy in the thirties, and real comfort could be derived from believing in rewards in *that* life since there were few in *this*. Although there was a growing class of educated people, even outside the Church and the universities, these institutions were guardians of the manuscripts and source of scribes to copy them. Schooling was in Latin, excluding all but a few, but on the other hand making it possible for those who knew it to correspond with scholars all over Europe.

With the revival of classical learning there was an increasing audience interested in reading about the classical past, the political and religious present, and the scientific future. Advances in the latter were rapid. Copernicus was born less than a generation after the Gutenberg Bible appeared. A system for distributing new information had already been established before that date.

While the Church remained very powerful, the corruption and dissension, the period of the two Popes, made it easy for people to question the right of its leaders to dictate all aspects of life. Once Luther nailed his 95 theses to the door in Wittenberg in 1517, the floodgates of doubt were opened (Small, 1982).

The stage was therefore set for the second great revolution in communication history after the invention of writing: the advent of printing. The Gutenberg Bible and Psalter were printed on six presses simultaneously and represent the first use of moveable, interchangeable parts and mass production with an assembly line procedure. It is estimated that within less than 50 years, over fifteen million volumes were produced by nearly 2,000 presses all over Europe except Russia. By 1530 there was a press in Mexico.

The production of multiple copies of a work meant that news travelled fast, that preservation was easier and censorship less effective, although it was first tried in England early in the sixteenth century and has been used frequently since. Within a decade after Luther's bold act, hundreds of thousands of copies of his writings were circulated all over Europe, making the reform movement widely known in a very short time. Within this period books were also published in pocket size and in the vernacular.

The goals and values of sixteenth- and seventeenth-century society were revealed in other ways, such as a new interest in developing systems for better organising the information which was becoming important, not only for the intellectuals, but also for the commercial groups. Until the seventeenth century alphabetising was little used, although it had been in the Alexandria Library. Gradually new systems of codifying and classifying material developed, aided by a sharp reduction in the price of paper. Encyclopedias became popular, followed by dictionaries, and by the middle of the seventeenth century scholarly journals were circulating.

The printing of books brought about other changes in society. Schooling became available to the new commercial classes, and, although the main subject was still Latin, mathematics and rhetoric also received attention. Reading was often first taught in the vernacular by means of spelling books.

Many new trades and professions developed and the people in them had greater access to power. Publishers were often among the best-educated people of their day with whom writers associated and consulted. Some of them fell victim to the Inquisition. Skilled printers, paper manufacturers and distributors, book designers and book sellers became important. Webster's speller, published in 1793, sold fourteen million copies by 1843 (Monaghan, 1983). Musicians churned out popular ballads, and writers such as Defoe set out to make money by writing books. Agents became active all over Europe, ferreting out all kinds of information such as financial news for Fugger's newsletter, or reporting the political news for the London and Edinburgh *Gazettes*, both started in the 1660s. In 1702 the first daily newspaper was published in London and seven years later there were 19 papers in London alone, feeding the information needs of increasing numbers of readers and capitalising on the shifts in society.

All of these developments in the two and a half centuries since printing began meant a great upheaval in society in general. Rabelais put it vividly not long after.

> I see robbers, hangmen, free-booters, tapsters, ostlers, and such like, of the very rubbish of the people, more learned now than the doctors and preachers were in my time. What shall I say? The very women and children have aspired to this praise and celestial Manna of good learning. (quoted by McLuhan, 1962, p.147)

The shifts in society reached a new height by the end of the eighteenth century with the American and French Revolutions. Both of these depended heavily on the printing press. Perhaps more important in terms of modern technological development were the accomplishments of Pascal, Newton, Leibnitz and Euler. They changed the way people looked at future events and ranked them, perceived light waves, saw the relationship between all matter, and discussed the theory of numbers. Boundaries of the European world also expanded with improved navigation and the colonial annexation of the New World and India.

The nineteenth century and the first decade of the twentieth saw the groundwork laid for information technology. Electricity was rapidly harnessed after Edison invented the light bulb in 1879, making many new kinds of what Bruner calls sensory extensions possible as well as an accelerated pace of scientific innovation. The study of eye movements while reading was one of these, leading to the publication of Huey's book on reading in 1908.

Mass publication of inexpensive books became common in the nineteenth century and specialised markets for romances or adventure stories were encouraged (Stern, 1980; Bonn, 1982). In business as in science, information became more and more valuable and the demand for ever faster transmission was not stilled by the invention of the telegraph, the telephone and the typewriter. With the industrial revolution in full swing, governments became involved in promoting and regulating nationwide systems such as the post office which required more data. While punched cards had already been used with some textile machinery, they were first used for government data collection in the United States census of 1890. A few years later the radio telephone was operating across the Atlantic and the electron tube was developed. Time and space had telescoped.

Computers and calculators of various kinds were built in the 1940s and by

1948 transistor devices were made. A year later Shannon and Weaver published *The Mathematical Theory of Communication*. The electronic age had begun. Not only did reading matter change, but the way it was stored and retrieved underwent equally great changes. In 1950 librarians joined mathematicians, psychologists, and linguists in documenting information processing procedures and uses, and the profession of being a librarian was altered in countless ways (Kent and Galvin, 1982; Mechler, 1982). Reading now reflects society's mad scramble for the latest information, and that is seen as access to power.

The harnessing of electricity and modern concepts of binary numbers were combined to produce a new means of coding information. The concepts of this combination have been important not only for encoding language, but for an understanding of all forms of encoding, including genetic. Information itself, in the new era, is defined as a reduction of uncertainty, and signals are all kinds of communications which reduce uncertainty. Natural processes such as the growth of corn or the birth of a baby are now seen by scientists as exchanges of information as well as biological processes (Ritchie, 1984). Information within the theory is not seen as synonymous with the traditional concept of *meaning* and the word is misleading (Sloman, 1978). Its value in the theory lies in the degree of uncertainty which precedes its reception – the greater the uncertainty, the greater the value of the information. Through Shannon's work and that of others, laws governing English text were elaborated and letter and word frequencies established. Table 1 is an example from Pierce's book, *Symbols, Signals and Noise: The Nature and Process of Communication*, written in the early electronic period, 1961.

Table 1

Word	Probability p	Code	Number of Digits in Code, N	Np
the	.50	1	1	.50
man	.15	001	3	.45
to	.12	011	3	.36
runs	.10	010	3	.30
house	.04	00011	5	.20
likes	.04	00010	5	.20
horse	.03	00001	5	.15
sells	.02	00000	5	.10
				2.26

Source: J. R. Pierce, *Symbols, Signals and Noise: The Nature and Process of Communication*. New York: Harper, 1961.

Reading in the electronic age, then, includes many varieties of encoding, decoding, and retrieval systems. The phonetic alphabet is only one of these. Neurophysiologists read brain scans, cardiologists read electrocardiograms, stock brokers read the Dow Jones report, now a century old, and sports addicts read the statistics of athletes. There are 'how to' books on everything from plumbing to meditation. Computers can draw maps from different angles and there are maps of the ocean floor. There is only one glaring problem: if people have not learned any of the coding systems, they cannot avail themselves of any of these delights. The goals and values of our society are reflected in tremendous disparity between those who can enjoy the fruits of the technological developments since the Gutenberg Bible and those left with the pips.

The teaching of reading is at the heart of formal education

Consideration of the disparity between those who can gain access to political and economic power through formal education and those who cannot is especially important for those who control the acquisition of symbolic code knowledge, which is at the heart of formal education. For, in spite of prophecies that traditional reading is a thing of the past, learning how to interpret a symbol system and the formal language which goes with it, and dealing with the 'decontextualised' nature of written language (Olsen, 1977; Stubbs, 1980; Martlew, 1983) is the modern equivalent of a working knowledge of Latin in the Renaissance. However, changes in emphasis in the teaching of reading are made necessary by the new technology and consequent changes in perception of society, the world, and the space around it. These perceptions, determined by our knowledge of and beliefs about the world, lead to mental representations of events which must then be related to words in order to communicate with others (Schank, 1982).

A few speculations follow about the kinds of changes that may be necessary in the teaching of reading in order to empower more elements of our society in the electronic age.

One of the changes is surely a renewed emphasis on probability thinking. Information theory assigns value to items of information by establishing how predictable they are; or the probability that they would occur. Artificial intelligence scholars, attempting to simulate human thought on the computer, have worked with this problem and with how much prior knowledge is necessary in order to increase the probability of predicting events, or making inferences. In studies of novices and experts, the latter have been proved far more able to make predictions and inferences by virtue of their internalised knowledge of a subject, which includes knowledge of the vocabulary or concepts, but also the possibilities or constraints within a particular structure of ideas (Greeno, 1980; Waldrop, 1984). While the emphasis at the beginning of the electronic age was on *process*, the *knowledge* of and experience with a certain area is now seen as central to comprehension. Knowledge is used in 'problem spaces' which include a variety of possible behaviours to be sorted out by search control knowledge acquired through past experience (Newell, 1980). The evidence points strongly to the need for instruction in probabilistic thinking based on specific facts and a familiarity with the structure of ideas related to those facts. A trained musician, familiar with the rules of classical music, knows that a dominant chord at the end of a sequence is likely to be followed by a tonic unless transition to another sequence is called for. In the thorough-bass period it was only necessary to write coded numbers below a melody. It seems quite clear that an endless series of true and false or multiple choice questions related to a text will never improve students' ability to think about probabilities and possibilities. Teacher/student dialogue is essential.

The structure of ideas within a particular field of knowledge is of course revealed by the language. Terry Winograd in *Language as a Cognitive Process, Volume I, Syntax* (1983) provides a masterful summary of the different ways in which the structure of language has been approached historically, reflecting the goals and values of each recent period. The point to be made here is that for each kind of information a special language is necessary prior knowledge for reading comprehension to take place. This necessary language includes cues as to the function of particular portions of text and to the special structure of ideas (Binkley, 1983).

Many of the cues to structure are of a visual nature (Gerhard, 1984) which is fortunate, since most people are able to see them and could be trained in what to look for. The visual form of text has undergone great transformations over the years, reflecting technological advances and changing the educational scene. Before printing, text was often beautifully illuminated, its function being to make each word important and to give the reader visual pleasure in the whole page. While there are still publishing companies which produce books with this in mind, the more common forms read today are newspaper columns, comics, advertisements, and a bewildering assortment of graphs, charts and models, as well as computer printouts of various kinds. A great deal of experience with and knowledge about the form, and the visual cues to the form, of these various ways of communicating information in print is needed for their comprehension. This seems to indicate necessary changes in the way goals are set up for students learning to read expository text and related forms. Something like search control knowledge should be emphasised, leading to the ability to predict where to look on a page for certain kinds of information. Visual training in shapes and configurations should not end with decoding instruction.

In expository text, but even more in the computer world, one structure of ideas to be revealed by visual search which is both basic and highly proble-matic is the category. Commands for both encoding and decoding on the computer require the assigning of information to a named class or category. While it is possible to memorise a limited number of procedures without understanding them, ultimately the reader must be aware of how the infor-mation is grouped. In top-down processing, category labels are given and accepted and subsequent information is grouped under them, or is seen as so grouped. In bottom-up processing, on the other hand, items of information are perceived first and are then seen to be related in different ways. Figures 1 and 2, to be read in the direction of the arrows, attempt to demonstrate these two ways of processing, as well as the relationship of these terms to the older ones of deduction and induction, and the Piagetian terms assimilation and accommodation.

Figure 1

Deduction – processing from generalisation to specific items
Assimilation – adding items to an existing category (structure)

TOP-DOWN PROCESSING

(A passage from a book on computer operations)
Some new ways of using old words in computer operations
  Breadboard: An early arrangement of a new electronic circuit so that
      it can be modified easily
  Bug and de-bug: Something is wrong with the system and needs to be
      put right
  Menu: A display on a screen of various options for action
  Graceful degradation: Something has gone wrong, but the computer
      manages to perform some operations
  Deadly embrace: All processes in the computer compete for the same
      resources and everything jams.

Source: R. I. Smith and B. Campbell, *Information Technology Revolution*. Harlow: Longman, 1981.

These two systems for processing language are given modern names, but they have been discussed since at least the time of Aristotle. They are significant in relation to the structure of society in that deductive thinking requires faith in some authority to assign category labels correctly, while induction makes enormous demands of the individual to make decisions alone, and implies faith in the ability of people to do this. Historically, formal rules for inductive thinking are very new and justification for individual empirical decisions is still a topic of controversy in philosophy (Luckenback,1972).

The ability to do bottom-up, inductive thinking is an important way of gaining access to power today. This way of processing information and its accompanying language grew out of the empirical sciences but spread to most fields, not least that of business management. The interpretation of a variety of facts in any area requires analysing similarities and differences between them, and the use of appropriate generalisations expressing the perceived relationship. This is also true of computer analysis, except that the rules for attributes have to be rigidly prescribed and do not allow for borderline cases (Sloman, 1978).

Four aspects of inductive thinking are especially relevant to a discussion of possible ways in which the emphasis within reading instruction needs to be changed in order to train students better for the electronic age. There is first the observational aspect. This requires people to hold their normal expectations, or mind set, in abeyance for the purpose of perceiving as objectively as possible. In science and the social sciences this often involves measurement or evaluation of various kinds. The purpose is to try to predict the probability of

Figure 2

'It seems to be a case of SOME NEW WAYS OF USING OLD
WORDS in some kind of communication system.'

Deadly embrace As in the sentence: 'Just when I was finishing the job,
there was a deadly embrace.'

Graceful degradation As in the sentence 'No, the system was not down
completely, but graceful degradation had set in.'

('This page seems to be about some kind of communication so these
words have something to do with information transmission.')

Menu As in the sentence: 'For some reason the menu did not include
SEARCH.'

('There must be some reason for using these words in such a peculiar
way. I wonder what this is about.')

Bug as in the sentence: 'I decided not to buy IGLOO because I heard
that it had too many bugs.'

Breadboard As in the sentence: 'Luckily we could change it because we
were still at the breadboard stage.'

(A passage from the remains of a magazine found in the dentist's waiting
room)

BOTTOM–UP PROCESSING

Accommodation – Forming a new, though related, category
Induction – Starting from single items, finding similarities, and moving
towards a generalisation expressing a relationship between
them

Source: See Figure 1.

an item of information, or an outcome, given a certain pattern of relationships; or projecting from the known to the unknown. Estimating the probability of an outcome is the second aspect of inductive thinking and is directly related to mathematical concepts, as is so much contemporary processing. To separate language totally from these concepts during instruction, or to associate mathematics exclusively with numbers, is not good preparation for the electronic age.

The third aspect of inductive thinking important to education is that for over a generation the total environment of a situation has been seen to affect any one item of information and its relationship to others, so that variables can no longer be legitimately ignored in favour of clean statements or research designs. Instead thinking needs to be holistic and evaluation often qualitative. This state of affairs has been arrived at because so many conclusions have been drawn which did not take the complexities of a situation into account and thus turned out to be erroneous, or because the time span used was far too short. This would seem to point to the need for more in-depth reading in the classroom, accompanied by analysis of all the elements affecting the subject matter; in a word, a more integrated approach to school subjects reflecting the changes in the real world.

Finally, if hypotheses are stated before a set of observations is made, may not the desire to prove or disprove them corrupt observation? This has certainly at time been the case. The dilemma arises when certainty rather than probability is the expected outcome (Nagel, 1955). While learning to frame hypotheses as a basis for investigating a topic is certainly useful, problem solving often requires seeing information in many different ways and different combinations, or flexibly. The ability to do this is crucial for innovative thinking.

All four aspects of inductive thinking discussed above require that educational systems provide a great deal of practice in *individual* processing of information; observing, making comparisons, and coming to appropriately phrased conclusions. These attempts should then not be judged necessarily right or wrong, but rather be the subject of discussion. It may be that our society comes to the conclusion that inductive thinking is not what is wanted of its citizens. In that case, piecemeal stabs at problem solving in the upper grades without any training in the lower grades should be abandoned in favour of sound deductive instruction. However, the disparity in access to power would inevitably widen.

Those who teach reading need a broad general education

The fourth point of this paper follows from the rest: those who teach reading need a broad general education in order to understand their society, the technological changes taking place which result in changes of perception and thinking processes, the role of language in all this, and the previous language experience and other experience to which students have been exposed, however limited it may be. Since learning consists of incorporating new information into existing frameworks while gradually altering and expanding these, nothing is to be gained by ignoring the reality of students' prior experience. The broad general education is especially needed if inductive thinking is to be encouraged. Teachers must be able to consider whether conclusions drawn by students follow logically from their observations, and whether they are couched in accurate and appropriate language. The large demands made by bottom-up, inductive processing require a very systematic way of approaching it and of making decisions.

The way in which teachers can help prepare their students for the more formal aspects of making decisions is indicated by an example from daily life taken from a recent book by Hurley on software decision making. The problem is to decide which coat to take to work or school in the morning. The text version of the problem is shown in Figure 3. Even in text form, the thinking process is set up for maximum clarity. What are the conditions, the possible actions, and the values of those actions? In matrix form (see Figure 4, page 20) the problem is even clearer, once the system is understood and the

Figure 3

Example from daily life

Conditions:	Is it raining and cold? Is it raining? (tests for the condition) Is it cold?	
Actions:	Wear lined raincoat Wear unlined raincoat Wear wool overcoat	(three possible and mutually exclusive actions)
Two values:	Yes No	
Exit:	Proceed to garage	

Source: R. B. Hurley, *Decision tables in software engineering*. New York: Van Nostrand Reinhold, 1983, p.10.

rules for making the decision, such as 'If it is both cold and raining, I shall take my lined raincoat', are formulated.

Seen in the light of an example from daily life, perhaps the idea of teaching to prepare students for the electronic age is less frightening and more related to the age of literate human beings than we thought. Children do work out *probabilities* of being punished for disobeying rules, they are able to talk about *conditions* for having a successful birthday party, the possible *actions* involved, and the *rules* to be made. They are also able to understand that a table has a certain *form* because of its *function*, that the *manner* in which a message or invitation is conveyed can affect the way it is received, and that there are limitations or *constraints* on the party due to space, time, and budgetary considerations. They know that the total *environment* can play a part in such ways as through an outbreak of chicken-pox, a storm, or a transportation strike. Finally, children know about *classifying* the guests in such ways as (1) those one wants to invite, (2) those one has to invite, (3) those who will bring delightful presents, or (4) those who will bring the discarded presents from their own party. Here are all the elements of decision-making and many of information processing ready to be built upon. Discussion of all of them will give opportunities to build up the necessary language, provided sufficient practice is allowed.

Teachers need to recognise and accept differences between their experience and that of their students

Our final point is that teachers in all ages have grown up under different historical conditions from their students, although not always as radically different as now, and that these differences need to be seen and accepted. This

Figure 4

Condition stub	Condition entry
Action stub	Action entry

Quadrants of a decision table.

	COAT TABLE	R1	R2	R3
C1	Raining	Y	Y	N
C2	Cold	Y	N	Y
A1	Wear lined raincoat	X		
A2	Wear unlined raincoat		X	
A3	Wear wool overcoat			X

Initial COAT TABLE showing the form of a decision table for some conditions, actions, and rules.

Source: R. B. Hurley, *Decision Tables in Software Engineering*. New York: Van Nostrand Reinhold, 1983, pp.7–8.

does not mean that they discard their experience as excess baggage, but rather that its relevance to contemporary developments needs to be explained. Comparing older and newer forms, subjects, symbols, and ways of communicating these can surely be a profitable exercise for all concerned, bringing the generations of literate and electronic mankind closer together, and offering golden opportunities for meaningful reading, and training in observation, comparison, and generalisation.

Conclusion

The tangible effects of the interaction between reading and technology include the many new ways in which information is visually presented or transmitted.

The basic purposes of communicating, however, are much the same as when writing was invented: speculating about cause and effect, offering goods for sale, recording transactions, reporting new developments, scheming against common enemies, and keeping in touch with friends. Technological inventions, therefore, can be seen even today as extensions of human capacities and as brought about by human needs.

Changes in the forms of communication have not come about through a one-way cause and effect process. Technology did not always suddenly arrive on the scene and cause a change in thinking and reading patterns. It has often been the other way around: new ideas, and combinations of ideas, arrived at by human beings through reading and writing activities, created a climate or a need for new technology because new possibilities were envisaged. Basic to technological progress has been the concept, however commercially and politically corrupted, that individual human beings are capable of making decisions and do not need intermediaries to their God, or to be dictated to by autocratic rulers or paternalistic employers.

The intangible effects of the interaction between reading and technology are less clear. In the electronic age technology threatens to widen the gap between those who have access to political and economic power and those who do not. Those of us committed to helping people gain access by becoming proficient in processing information need to take into account its changing nature, different use of language, and the kinds of mental representations which will be needed for proper selection of stimuli. As William James said in 1890,

> My experience is what I agree to attend to. Only those items which I *notice* shape my mind – without selective interest, experience is an utter chaos. (*Principles of Psychology*, pp.284–5)

Reading and technology: tangibles and intangibles

A highly selective list of interesting events related to reading and technology

1000 BC	Phonetic spelling transmitted to the Greeks
350 BC	All Greek states adopt the 24-letter alphabet
100 BC	Alexandria Library reputed to hold 700,000 manuscripts
200 AD	Ptolemy draws world map with latitude and longtitude
700	Moorish invasion of Spain: Arabic numerals and algebra introduced in Europe
1190	Paper mills operating in France
1200	Compass known to be in use in many parts of the world
1325–50	Introduction of fire arms in Europe
1346	Division of hours and minutes into 60s
1440s	Moveable type invented: first use of standardised, interchangeable parts and assembly line operations
1456	Gutenberg Bible printed on six presses simultaneously

1500	Nearly 2,000 printing presses in Europe print 15–20 million volumes
	Books printed in the vernacular
	First pocket books printed in Venice
1504	Beginning of restrictions on printing in England
1517	Luther's theses posted in Wittenberg, disseminated all over Europe by 1525
1522	First arithmetic books printed in England
1530	Printing press established in Mexico
1565	Invention of lead pencils
1585	Decimal system developed
1588	Alphabet system of teaching reading through spelling known
1610	Galileo sees Jupiter through telescope he made
1614–20	Napier develops logarithmic tables
1650	Pascal writes about the laws of probability, uses calculating machine
	Beginning of scholarly journals
1702	Daily newspaper published in London
1725	Stereotype invented by Scottish goldsmith, William Ged
1731	Sextant invented by John Hadley
1783	Publication of Webster's speller; 14 million copies sold by 1843
1796	Invention of lithograph process
	Paper made from pulp rather than rags
1814	*The Times* of London printed on the first flat-bed cylinder press powered by steam (1,100 impressions per hour)
1822	Niepce produced first photograph
1840s	Mass publication of inexpensive books
1850	Engraving on metal by photographic means
1860s	Colour printing process developed
1866	*The Times* printed on rotary press using both sides of continuous roll of paper (25,000 impressions per hour)
1870	Compulsory Education Act in England, 1872 in Scotland
1873–84	Development of telegraphy, the telephone, the phonograph, the typewriter, Waterman's fountain pen
	Eye movements analysed
	Set theory developed by George Cantor
1879	Edison invents the light bulb
1885	Linotype patented
1890	Punched data cards used for U.S. census
1897	Influence of expectation on perception of words studied
1900–2	Automatic stereotype plates
	Transmission of photographs by wire
	Trans-Atlantic radio telephone (Herz, Marconi)
1903	Wright brothers' flight

1905	Einstein's theory of relativity
1900–10	Rapid development of electron tubes
1927–29	Television used in a laboratory
	Use of teletype
1940s	Development of different computers, calculators
1948	Development of transistor devices
1950	Librarians join mathematicians, psychologists, linguists etc. in documenting information processing procedures and uses
1956	Term 'artificial intelligence' coined
1961	Russians launch space ship
1962	Post Office communications station established to track satellites, transmit and receive signals
1970	Post Office publishes telephone directory printed by an integrated computer process
1979	Prestel, based in London, was the first public viewdata service
1969–81	Decisions against restrictions imposed by AT&T encouraged competition in communications industry

References

BINKLEY, M. (1983) A descriptive and comparative study of cohesive structure in text materials from differing academic disciplines. Unpublished dissertation. Washington, D.C.: George Washington University.

BONN, T. L. (1982) *Undercover: An Illustrated History of American Mass Market Paperbacks*. Harmondsworth: Penguin.

BRUNER, J. S. (1965) 'Growth of mind'. *American Psychologist*, 20, pp.1007–17

BRUNER, J. S., OLVER, R. R. and GREENFIELD, P. M. (1966) *Studies in cognitive Growth*. New York: Wiley.

EISENSTEIN, E. L. (1979) *The Printing Press as an Agent of Change: Communications and Cultural Transformations in Early-modern Europe*, Volume 1. Cambridge: C.U.P.

FULLER, R. B. (1981) *Critical Path*. New York: St Martin's.

GERHARD, C. (1984) 'Meeting student need to understand structure in expository text', in D. Dennis (ed) *Reading: Meeting Children's Special Needs*. London: Heinemann.

GREENO, J. G. (1980) 'Trends in the theory of knowledge for problem solving', in D. T. Tuma and F. Reif (eds) *Problem Solving and Education: Issues in Teaching and Research*. Hillsdale, N. J.: Erlbaum.

HUEY, E. B. (1968, originally published 1908) *The Psychology and Pedagogy of Reading*. Cambridge, Mass.: M.I.T.

HURLEY, R. B. (1983) *Decision Tables in Software Engineering*. New York: Van Nostrand Reinhold.

JAMES, W. (1890) *Principles of Psychology*. New York: Holt.

KENT, A. and GALVIN T. (eds) (1982) *Information Technology: Critical Choices for Library Decision-makers*. New York: Marcel Edkker.

LUCKENBACK, S. A. (ed) (1972) *Probabilities, Problems, and Paradoxes: Readings in Inductive Logic*. Belmont, Calif.

McLUHAN, M. (1962) *The Gutenberg Galaxy: The Making of Typographical Man*. Toronto: University of Toronto.

MARTLEW, M. (1983) *The Psychology of Written Language: Developmental and Educational Perspectives*. New York: Wiley.

MECHLER, A. M. (1982) *Micropublishing: A History of Scholarly Micropublishing in America 1938-1980*. Westport, Conn.: Greenwood.

MONAGHAN, E. J. (1983) *A Common Heritage: Noal Webster's Blue-Back Speller*, Hamden, Conn.: Archon Books.

MUKERJI, C. (1983) *From Graven Images: Patterns of Modern Materialism*. New York: Columbia University.

NAGEL, E. (1955) 'Principles of the theory of probability'. *International Encyclopedia of Unified Science*, 1, pp.343-422.

NEWELL, A. (1980) 'Reasoning, problem solving, and decision processes: the problem space as a fundamental category'. In R. S. Nickerson (ed) *Attention and Performance, Volume 3*. Hillsdale, N. J.: Erlbaum.

OLSON, D. R. (1977) 'From utterance to text: the bias of language in speech and writing'. *Harvard Educational Review*, 47, pp.257-81.

ONG, W. J. (1977) *Interfaces of the Word: Studies in the Evolution of Consciousness and Culture*, Ithaca, N. Y.: Cornell.

PIERCE, J. R. (1961) *Symbols, Signals, and Noise: The Nature and Process of Communication*. New York: Harper.

RITCHIE, D. (1984) *The Binary Brain: Artificial Intelligence in the Age of Electronics*. Boston: Little, Brown.

SCHANK, R. (1982) *Reading and Understanding: Teaching from the Perspective of Artificial Intelligence*. Hillsdale, N. J.: Erlbaum.

SCHOLZ, T. W. (ed) (1983) *Decision Making Under Uncertainty*. New York: North-Holland.

SCRIBNER, S. and COLE, M. (1981) *The Psychology of Literacy*. Cambridge, Mass.: Harvard University.

SHANNON, C. E. and WEAVER, W. (1964, originally published 1949) *The Mathematical Theory of Communication*. Urbana, Ill.: University of Illinois.

SLOMAN, A. (1978) *The Computer Revolution in Philosophy: Philosophy Science, and Models of Mind*. New Jersey: Humanities Press.

SMALL, C. (1982) *The Printed Word: An Instrument of Popularity*. Aberdeen: Aberdeen University.

SMITH, R. I. and CAMPBELL, B. (1981) *The Information Technology Revolution*. Harlow: Longman.

STERN, M. B. (ed) (1980) *Publishers for Mass Entertainment in Nineteenth Century America*. Boston: G. K. Hall.

STUBBS, M. (1980) *Language and Literacy: The Sociolinguistics of Reading and Writing*. London: Routledge & Kegan Paul.

WALDROP, M. M. (1984) 'Artificial intelligence (I): into the world'. *Science*, February pp.802-5.

WALDROP, M. M. (1984) 'The necessity of knowledge'. *Science*, March, pp.1279-82.

WINOGRAD, T. (1983) *Language as a Cognitive Process, Volume I, Syntax*, Reading, Mass.: Addison-Wesley.

2 The book in 2000

Martyn Goff

The scene is a Russian railway station, 240 miles east of Moscow. A train stands at the platform about to leave, the platform itself thronged with people seeing off relatives and friends. Just as the first whistles blow, three men, two tall and thin and one short and fat, dash up to the ticket office where the booking clerk is drawing tea from a samovar. They shout that the train is going and will he please serve them. He does, and they dash on to the platform as the train begins to pull out. The two tall men run for all they are worth and manage to board a coach three from the end. The short, fat man just – but only just – reaches the brass handle on the very last carriage, holds on for a moment, and then, as the train gathers speed, drops helplessly on to the platform.

He can be seen huddled and shaking and, as people rush to his aid, is thought to be sobbing. Only, when they reach him they find to their amazement that he is laughing for all he is worth. 'But why', they demand, 'are you laughing, having missed the train?' 'Those two' he splutters, pointing after the train disappearing into the distance, 'those two – they only came to see me off!'

The pertinence of that story to my paper is simply that I have come aboard among the most impressive group of experts on reading that I have ever encountered at one go and feel myself to be only an admiring, amateur onlooker.

For many years now, despite universal education, at least in developed countries, the problems of reading and of learning to read have seemed considerable if not enormous. We still talk of millions of semi-literates or reluctant readers, even in highly industrialised countries. Suddenly, now these problems are totally overshadowed by a very much greater one: the arrival of the new technologies which threaten, at least in some of their own makers' eyes, to make reading obsolescent. In 1979, Dr Christopher Evans in his book, *The Mighty Micro*, wrote: 'In sum, the 1980s will see the book as we know it, and as our ancestors created and cherished it, begin a slow but steady decline into oblivion.' Much of the earlier chapters of that book are in similar vein, though it is worth noting that on the back of the jacket, Dr Evans was photographed in a book-lined study!

Of course, Dr Evans had been preceded by Professor McLuhan by some years, the same Professor McLuhan who foretold the end of the book. After all, he claimed: 'the medium is the message'.

Dr Evans's 1980s are almost half-way through and the number of books sold is increasing everywhere. Professor McLuhan, in a letter to me only months before his death, wrote:

There have been indications of TV saturation among many high school students. That tends to mean that they have undergone considerable depletion of psychic resources before reaching this stage of apathy.... The main effect of television is loss of identity and its ensuing violence.

However, *my* message is that the book not only is going to survive the new technology but is going to continue to grow in importance. I base such a bold statement not on Dr Evans's having clearly been wrong in his time scale, nor on Marshall McLuhan's retraction of his former beliefs. My reasons for believing in the future of the book are wider and more complex than those two simple facts.

Perhaps, first, we can deal with the prophets of doom who always see every new thing as incorporating a death sentence on its predecessors. Dan Boorstin, the Librarian of Congress, has shown us quite clearly that, whereas new art forms and new means of retrieving information are always initially seen as dispossessing their forerunners, they almost always end only by modifying them. For example, the coming of photography was seen as the end of painting. But what happened in fact was that by largely removing from painting its principal task of recording – faces, groups, houses, ships and so on – it freed that art in a way that led to abstract painting, surrealism, cubism, vorticism and the like. Painting is as strong today as ever, even though photography itself is now considered as an art form.

Similarly the gramophone record was seen as the end of the live concert, whereas in fact it turned out to be the biggest propaganda element for those concerts. Records converted millions to music and still made those millions want to hear their favourite artists in the flesh. The radio was to have been the end of newspapers, and then in itself was going to be superseded by the arrival of television. But newspapers are alive and fairly healthy despite both those media of communication, and radio has blossomed into all sorts of new fields: local radio stations, CB radio and so forth. The relation of newspapers on the one hand and television and radio on the other is in fact a clue to the importance of the written word. We see an item of news on television or hear about it on the radio, but for deeper, considered views – for *knowledge* as against *information* – we turn to newspapers where those items are analysed in depth: at least in *The Times* and the *Guardian* if not in the *Sun*. Thus there is no necessary logical step whereby the arrival of television and computers and video recorders and the like will put an end to the book. While obviously much information retrieval will be switched to those new technologies, the technologies themselves need accompanying books. (I recently bought a marvellous radio. I can set it searching for the station I want; I can dial in the number of kilohertz and it will find the station I want in seconds; it will wake me up and play a programme which I had fed into its memory days earlier. And so on. But without the voluminous book of instructions that radio would have been as useless to me as without its batteries!)

It might be as well to summarise here some other practical points about the book that constitute in small part its superiority. First, the book is cheap. Before you start throwing £15 biographies at me, let me remind you of what you get for a £1 or £1.95 paperback. And whereas that £15 spent on a meal lasting an hour or so is soon forgotten, the book is always there to be read. It may be an eight or ten hour experience; re-read; lent to someone else or to many others and if returned, which doesn't always happen, put on a shelf to become one of the most delightful forms of furniture and decoration that exist.

Second, the book is amazingly portable. It can be carried anywhere: on a train, a plane, a beach, in a park, into a bath. In some of those places you can take a radio or portable television, or a tape recorder, but not by any means all.

Third, a book is flexible. You can fail to get the meaning of a sentence; put your finger or a bit of paper in that page and read on, flick back and forth between that and other pages until the meaning becomes clear. It can be done a thousand times more easily than the same operation with tape or video cassette.

Four, book reading is wonderfully private. If just one person in a group were to switch on a hi-fi or television set, everyone's aural attention would be trespassed upon. But every single one could be reading a different book in a hall at the same moment without disturbing anyone else. And we live, as a society, in smaller and smaller homes with smaller and smaller rooms.

But these are minor, practical advantages. However real they may be, they are not why the book will continue to exist alongside the new technologies. Let us begin to look at some of the deeper implications of the continuing importance of the book.

First is a minor one. George Steiner once said: 'I go into a bookshop for the book I didn't know I wanted.' In the same way a great deal of my own education was acquired quite accidentally through books. For example, when looking up a specific word in a dictionary, my eye took in, and learnt, two or three more. Given an essay to read by one of my teachers, my eye caught another – *Two Cheers for Democracy* by E. M. Forster – and it was this other that had a profound and lasting effect on my outlook and ideals. This form of serendipity is a powerful stimulant to acquiring both information and knowledge painlessly and pleasurably.

Second, we read a book at our own pace not at that of the television producer. Barbara Tuchman, the American historian, said in a lecture at the Library of Congress in October 1979:

The essential nature of TV is that its program is designed not for self-expression but to sell something other than itself to the greatest number of viewers. Books, being self-selected by the consumer, can keep pace with his growing maturity in age and taste, whereas the media on the whole must remain at a level that its programmers believe palatable to the widest possible audience. . . . Books by their heterogeneity can never represent a managed culture, whereas the airwaves by their nature and control by licensing might.

Two points are there, well worth stressing: one is that everyone can read the same book at a different pace. In transmitted programmes, the pace is dictated and is often cast at the level of the lowest. Second, and more important, is that the new technologies can be controlled in a way that is impossible via the book. 'Books', to repeat Barbara Tuchman's words, 'can never represent a managed culture.'

Those of us who read easily and fluently, and I refer of course, to the world at large, not a specialised audience of experts with their very special understanding of what reading constitutes for a human being, can easily take the significance of reading for granted. As Margaret Meek says in her book, *Learning to Read*:

> Can you really imagine what life would be like if you had never learned to read? The special disadvantages – not being able to read street signs or notices in the post office – are easy to understand. But what about encounters with new ideas?

Every day we come across some extraordinary new example of contemporary technology: a phone that tells a retailer whether a customer's credit card can be used for a given sum if the card is dropped into a slot in the phone and a certain number dialled; an on-line computer that tells us how many free seats there are in an aircraft still 6,000 miles away; a light pen that reads a minute ticket on an object being sold and alters stock records and re-orders instantly. And yet ... and yet ... the people operating these modern marvels are every bit as liable to misunderstandings with their colleagues as their forerunners in the steam age ever were. Those misunderstandings arise from imprecise or ambivalent use of words, or words remain the way in which we talk to each other, inform each other, program each other; and words are learnt and understood, words are *felt*, by reading.

It might be apposite here to intersperse a thought on a question which might arise. Television, we are often told, is not anti-book or anti-words; on the contrary it stimulates an interest in both. Not only do many programmes originate in a book, but when, for example, *The Forsyte Saga* and *The Raj Quartet* were televised in serial forms, sales of the books shot up. But research does not support this argument. The Independent Broadcasting Authority's own findings are quite unambivalent about this:

> Television has not really functioned as a stimulus to reading, but as a substitute on a really widespread scale. ... Of those small numbers, and 3% is the largest figure yet recorded, who have bought or obtained works after seeing TV adaptations, a noticeable proportion have clearly not finished reading them.

The *Daily Telegraph*, in an article on the subject in 1983, suggested delinquency arises from an atrophied facility for fantasy, and that it is no coincidence that the delinquency rate has increased in those Western societies which have moved from the influence of fiction and radio drama to that of television, which 'instantly gratifies our senses'. How interesting, indeed, that the conclusions of the newspaper writer should be matched by those of Marshall McLuhan which I quoted above.

I will return for a moment to Margaret Meek and quote her again:

It is also important to realise that not all the electronic media in the world will replace what happens when a reader meets a writer. Reading is the active encounter of one mind and one imagination with another. Talk happens; the words fly, remembered or not. Writing remains; we read it at our own pace which is the rate of *our* thinking. Real reading cannot be done without thought. As it is a kind of inner speech, it is bound to have a marked effect on the growth of the mind of the reader.

A failure to read thus affects a person not only in terms of human communication, but also in terms of the development of his or her mind. Nowhere is this truer, of course, than when we are talking about the young.

To communicative and imaginative impoverishment we must also add emotional impoverishment if we allow reading to be replaced by the new technologies.

Jung has told us of 'race memories' and their importance to the human mind and soul. The inherent greatness of myth and fairy tale is its poetic greatness. Leon Garfield and Edward Blishen in *The God Beneath the Sea* remind us that: 'The human experience brought to mind by myth and fairy tale extends beyond the situation described by psychologists and anthropologists. It is conscious as well as unconscious, and civilised as well as primitive.'

The child who is deprived of having fairy stories and myths read aloud is a child lacking in an important dimension of his or her possible development. It is no good us mouthing easy words about the quality of life, as we now do so often and so ineffectively, unless we understand what we are doing if we deprive children of a source of feeling about their emotional development that is imprinted in them as they listen to or are read myths and fairy stories. *No branch of the new technology can provide a substitute for this*.

Jerome Singer, Professor of Psychology at Yale University, has shown us that the 'cognitive revolution' of the past few decades has demonstrated that 'we have at least two major systems for processing information for restructuring it within our memory. One system has been called lexical and involves sequences of words usually organised into dictionary-like hierarchies. The second system relates to the specific representation of events we have seen, heard, touched, tasted or smelled.' Carl Pribram, of the University of California, in confirming that the lexical system is primarily related to the left side of the brain and imagery to the right, has suggested that neglect of the left-hand side may actually lead to the atrophy of the development and well-being of that half of the brain. Its food is words; and the child starved of enough words, starved of books, will actually be less well equipped, less rounded, less able a child than the one who is a constant reader.

It was Carl Pribram, too, who commented on a theory of Julian James about the change in human consciousness by saying. 'I think that the change came about with the invention of writing. Once one writes something down, one has the chance to validate it through consequential means, that is with other people.' A sudden change in human development which led to this sort of print and word training being precipitately cut off could lead to severe with-drawal symptoms; thus my use above of the word 'atrophy'.

Jacob Timmermans was flung into a South American jail by the dictator of the country where he lived, for publishing a book. He asked that same dicta-tor, when he was eventually released after years of imprisonment and torture, why he had not been treated in that way when he was every day bringing out a national newspaper expressing the same views. 'Because', answered the dictator, 'a book has a life of its own. A newspaper can be silenced, confis-cated, pressured or won over with threats. If the journalists' articles are not published, their writing has no importance. Furthermore, if they are not going to be published, they won't get written in the first place. But books are written, whether or not they are published at the moment or in the place they are written. They have a secure destiny. A manifest destiny. A lasting exis-tence.'

I will quote Margaret Meek yet again: 'To be literate in the civic or material sense of belonging to a literate society is to be able not only to read but also to question the authority of even the most official-looking document that makes demands on us.' This is surely only another way of saying, as Barbara Tuchman did: 'Books by their heterogeneity can never represent a managed culture, whereas the airwaves by their nature and control by licensing might.'

It is worth adding that, in the light of this, the real threat to the child from the world of the new technology is multiplied because these pressures are being most strongly applied and felt at an age when the child is already finding his or her leisure time facing strong competition. School work, puberty and a host of new interests loudly jostle for attention in the 11 to 13 age bracket. It is up to us to devise ways of making sure that deprivation to which I referred above is never allowed to become total. Neither 'Coronation Street' nor 'Crossroads', nor standing in W. H. Smith playing computer games on the display machines, will provide the food that comes from reading books that stimulate the imagination and inform and furnish the mind.

Nor does what I have said about human beings' imagination apply only to children. If I were to show a film starring Richard Burton and Elizabeth Taylor, every one of us would see those two people in almost the same way. But if we were able to read a story in which the two characters played by those actors were described by the author, then every one of us would flesh out those characters in a slightly different way; in other words, we would bring into play our personal and individual imaginative abilities.

I have shown a number of reasons, by no means exhaustive, why I think the book remains as important as ever despite the arrival of all the new tech-nology. I have also shown that in simple practical terms it is as remarkable as any of the new inventions we brag about. Stop and marvel for a moment at the number of words in a pocket dictionary; the amount of history or philosophy compressed into a few hundred pages that can be contained in a pocket book; and the influence to this day of a single book like the Bible. But my aim is to hazard some not uninformed guesses about how far the book would be displaced by the new technology. Society doesn't necessarily accept what is good for it: if it did, no doubt *The Times* would vastly outsell the *Sun*. The book may be desirable for humankind, but – faced by the barrage of extremely skilful, highly financed propaganda telling us that the computer and television and any number of combinations of the two will be all that we need for communication and entertainment in the future – will we not turn our backs on books completely? My answer still remains NO.

I have already indicated that an area of information retrieval will pass from the book to the new technology: that is inevitable and welcome. But against that we must set the almost certainty that the present balance between work and leisure will change at first gradually and then more swiftly in the next few years. As robots replace people in every sense, we will need to work perhaps three days a week, to begin with, then maybe two: the working week and the week-end will change places in time span. That leisure will need filling; and for many it will need filling creatively; the book will be one of the ways of doing it. If Marshall McLuhan is right and we shall all begin to suffer from TV saturation, then the turn back to the book may be even greater. I foresee then for the book a reasonably golden future. The use of the word 'reasonably', the speck of doubt that makes me employ it, relates to one factor only: that children continue to be taught to read in a way that *sui generis* makes reading a pleasure. No one doubts for a second the vital importance of learning to read: would only that that view prevailed with equal certainty everywhere.

I have left till last one branch of the book that has a function in our society of the greatest importance; one which, in the face of a world seemingly hell-bent on its own destruction, becomes more important as day succeeds day. I refer, of course, to literature. Long after we have forgotten the names of Generals and Prime Ministers, Kings and Queens, those of the greatest artistic creators remain household words. Who was the Elector of Bavaria in Beethoven's time? Or, closer to home, Sovereign in Shakespeare's? If the arts are one of the few glories of human society to date, then literature shares with music and painting the forefront. I believe that our writers are as vital to society as ever they were. Over sixty years ago R. G. Collingwood wrote:

> The artist must prophesy, not in the sense that he foretells things to come, but in the sense that he tells his audience, at the risk of their displeasure, the secrets of their own hearts. His business as an artist is to speak out, to make a clean breast. But what he has to utter is not, as the individualistic theory of art would have us think, his own secrets. As spokesman of his community, the secrets he must utter are theirs. The reason why they need him is that no community altogether knows its own heart; and by failing in this knowledge a community deceives itself on the one subject concerning which ignorance means death. For the evils which come from that ignorance the poet as prophet suggests no remedy, because he has already given one. The remedy is the poem itself. Art is the community's medicine for the worst disease of the mind, the corruption of consciousness.

I believe that the book *is* here to stay; I believe that literature *must* stay. Our futures, the quality of the society in which we live, depend in part on this. Ernest Boyer said:

31

The more we use computers, the more dependent on them we become. Their importance can only increase. And yet THEY WILL NOT REPLACE THE BOOK. Knowledge is not synonymous with data, and the sort of knowledge found in most books is simply not suitable for electronic storage. Data is accumulating in all areas with such speed that computers are essential to house it for future sorting and use, but unfortunately we are not accumulating knowledge – and certainly not wisdom – at anywhere near the same rate.

'Art', I quoted from Collingwood, 'is the community's medicine for the worst disease of the mind, the corruption of consciousness.' 'Computers', said Ernest Boyer, 'will not replace the book.' In the combination of those two thoughts lies the answer to the question: will the book survive in the face of new technology? My answer is a resounding YES.

References

BOYER, ERNEST (1981) 'The Book and Education'. Essay from *The State of the Book World 1980*. Washington: Library of Congress.

COLLINGWOOD, R. G. (1923) *Art Now*. Oxford: O.U.P.

EVANS, CHRISTOPHER (1979) *The Mighty Micro*. London: Gollancz.

GARFIELD, LEON and BLISHEN, EDWARD (1970) *The God Beneath the Sea*. Harlow: Longman.

INDEPENDENT BROADCASTING AUTHORITY (1980) 'Fiction and Depiction'. *IBA 1980 Report*. London: Independent Broadcasting Authority.

MEEK, MARGARET (1982) *Learning to Read*. London: Bodley Head.

PRIBRAM, KARL (1970) *Biology of Memory*. London: Academic Press.

SINGER, JEROME (1981) *Television Imagination and Agression*. N.J.: Erlbaum.

TIMERMANS, JACOB (1982) *Prisoner Without a Name*. Harmondsworth, Middx: Penguin.

TUCHMAN, BARBARA (1981) *The Book*. Washington: Library of Congress.

3   Reading and the new technologies: the role for teacher training

J. G. Morris

In the last five years in the United Kingdom there has been a drive to introduce microelectronics and associated technology into the educational system. This drive is in two parts: one is associated with England, Wales and Northern Ireland in an organisation called the Microelectronics in Education Programme (M.E.P.), and the second is a Scottish group called the Scottish Microelectronics Development Programme (S.M.D.P.). The former has a four to six year lease of life and then devolves its activities upon 14 regional centres; the latter is a permanent organisation although it too has 11 regional satellites. The reason for having two separate bodies need not concern us greatly here. Both began under educational auspices and had the usual justifications or postulated programmes of computer awareness, curriculum development, help for the handicapped, administration and assessment.

Education departments in the United Kingdom now make the proverbial church mouse appear affluent. Education itself is the god that failed because, in a country where people are swimming about trying to understand how they got into their present difficulties, someone or something has to be the scapegoat. Traditionally those in greatest danger have been gods and messengers. In the absence of messengers we turned on the gods.

If the education departments had been left to their own initiatives I imagine that both programmes would have chuntered on slowly with very little new money being available but with plenty of exhortations being sent out from the central authorities in badly written circulars and memoranda. At a relatively early stage two upstarts joined in the game and brought their own balls. One was the Manpower Services Commission with its get-up-and-go-attitude and its demand for relevance related to training and employment. The accent was vocational. A parallel may be seen in the nineteenth-century industrial schools. The second Johnnie-come-lately was the Department of Trade and Industry. Its motivation was and is to develop British industry with a view to having a sound export market and therefore more jobs in the home market.

These two newcomers put a considerable amount of money forward but it was earmarked for specific use. They stressed hardware and training. They made noises about software but were more vague in their intentions here. One result has been that some 80 per cent of the educational effort in the U.K. is locked into the B.B.C. Model B microcomputer and the makers, Acorn, have been given a further four-year contract. This is a very different situation from that found in educational circles in Europe, America, Japan, Australia and Canada.

I would like to make two pairs of distinctions. The first distinction is between hardware-led development and curriculum-led development. Our educational history over a long period of time has shown us that only curriculum-led development will incorporate and stimulate hardware. It does not seem to work the other way round.

The second pair of distinctions is between hard and soft technology. The hard technology is the microcomputer with its peripherals and with its systems program, i.e. what makes the microcomputer run. The other is soft technology which is applications programs for the various makes of microcomputers related to the various languages used, but it is also such things as having theories, identifying communication techniques which work in education, drawing up plans to meet objectives, making judgements and showing the logic of how we move from the decision to the objective. This is the soft technology which has been neglected.

Why computers at all?

It is said that mountaineers when asked why they climb a mountain reply, 'Because it is there.' I have never heard any mountaineer say this. It could be that if they say it they are merely being polite because they are all followers of Bertrand Russell who insisted that: 'Why questions cannot be answered.' Thus it is hard to answer the question of, 'Why computers at all?' There is no way of stopping the tide of them in schools at present and there is even less chance of stopping the tide of them for the home. I refer to the nasty little ones which are readily available in all the high street shops. We have the phenomenon of the sale of the *Encyclopaedia Britannica* now in electronic form driven by the same force, that of parents who wish to do the best they can for their children and accept the line that a child will be handicapped without a microcomputer at home.

I have used the term 'tide' related to schools but even with the very considerable sums of public money which have been spent we are still at the stage of a handful of microcomputers in schools. My own view, and it is a ballpark figure, is that one micro to six pupils is about right if the micro is going to be an accepted and used educational feature in schools. I know of no school in the U.K. with more than 50 microcomputers and even then they are a job lot; that is, they lack compatibility.

There is also the problem of the language. Nearly all pupils in our schools use Basic. This is a high level language but one which the *cognoscenti* love to hate. Its advantages are that it minimises the need to understand editing, compiling, loading/linking and execution. It is easy but slow. You can only edit by using line numbers; often you have to retype the whole line and there are limited program structuring capabilities. List structures are not available. There are many variations of Basic and almost anything I say can be challenged by a particular variation but in broad terms the pros and cons I have listed are correct. The real computer buff would demand Pascal as the appropriate language. There are two other groups the one favouring authoring languages and the other favouring Logo. For authoring languages I would say that they require a great deal of store but more important they lock you into a methodology of teaching which may not be the most appropriate one for a particular subject. The inventor of Logo says that it is 'a philosophy of education relating to a family of languages'. Suffice to say that in the educational field of using the microcomputer there are groups of people strongly prejudiced for or against specific languages. The classification would be that Basic is a procedural language whereas Prolog and Lisp are the declarative languages. The latter merely means that the computer can make its own relationships once it knows about the rules.

At present a fourth-generation computer can make 100,000 logical inferences per second, and those who promise the fifth-generation microcomputer aim to have 100 million such inferences per second. That seems a lot but the human brain is a mass of cells which can make one and 800 nothings after it relationships. 'Whaur's yer micro noo?' This brings me on to language, a very suitable theme for this Conference. Some will genuinely fail to understand that sentence. Others will affect not to understand it. The United Kingdom as a relatively small island has people who specialise in failing to understand anyone who lives more than 50 miles from where they are. It is common when a Scottish play appears on network television for people from the south of England to demand sub-titles. They make very little effort to understand and they are arrogant enough to give the impression that they are able to read. Even if we could overcome human intransigence, we are still left with the problem of ambiguity, metaphor, word order and emphasis all of which make it improbable that natural language will be a way of accessing the computer for rather a long time yet. Britain, Japan and the U.S.A. are all engaged in research on the fifth generation in micro. They may succeed but I still remember efforts to translate Lincoln and Churchill into machine language.

Teacher training

It is time to come to the heart of my topic but this rather long yet superficial introduction is essential to ensure that we are all at the same baseline, a vitally important feature of computing in education.

There are about 600,000 people earning their living in the United Kingdom under the omnibus title of 'teacher'. Currently a very small number are coming on stream as new teachers. The numbers in the colleges of education have slumped dramatically over the last few years. Thus the first question must be to maintain the value of your capital, i.e. the teachers already in the field. The obvious solution to this is 'in-service training', a slogan which can be used to cure everything from dandruff to in-growing toe nails and all points in between. It is certainly honoured in the breach. Valiant efforts are made to provide in-service training for this huge teaching force but most of them manage to avoid it quite successfully despite the mass of conferences which break out like a rash at the beginning and end of all the statutory holiday periods. At least they recycle the money to help maintain halls of residence out of term time. Unless these teachers in service are given the opportunity to feel secure with microelectronics and the new technologies, they will not represent fertile ground for new teachers going out into the schools from colleges. I have used the term new technologies and should perhaps describe it. For me it is:

(a) microcomputers and direct peripherals with their attendant competencies;
(b) electronic devices which can be self-programmed;
(c) concept keyboards;
(d) interactive video;
(e) distribution, retrieval and communication systems based on land-line, broadcasting or other forms of transmission.

My thesis is that knowledge of these technologies by itself cannot possibly be successful unless there is a radical change in teacher training, both pre-service and in-service. I also think this is unlikely to happen for two reasons. The first is that the U.K.'s college of education system is now staffed by demoralised people who require therapy themselves. The second is that teachers maintain their security in our educational system by pre-determining the subject and lesson content and also often by holding back the class with a wall of talk, or in the very liberal places by a wall of activity. There is a need to distinguish activity and action.

My thesis is that the microcomputer can be assimilated into school education if it is used to handle all the routine work in learning. We can argue about what is routine. This leaves the teacher free to keep the ring, be available for consultation and to handle seminars. Very few teachers indeed are able to sustain such a system. They would have to cease to be founts of knowledge and be learners along with their pupils but having rather more experience of where and how to find out. For most teachers this would be too big a risk. The other aspect which tends to be taken for granted is that there are thousands of pupils out there just thirsting for knowledge. Not so. Teachers themselves will only use the system advocated if they are exposed to it in their pre-service and in-service courses and this again makes very great demands upon those in the colleges and institutes of education. Whoever does the planning has to try to answer at least five questions; that I shall now try to do.

Question 1. *Whom to train?*

The immediate and simplistic answer is teachers already in service. The word teacher covers a great number of types of person working in education, from the probationer in primary school to the head teacher of a large secondary school. Should the selection be based on key people and, if so, how are they identified? Can you get a multiplier effect by training a few people in one school and, if so, what is the minimum number of teachers to be trained in any institution for it to have a noticeable effect? Should teachers be trained on the basis of their subjects or is there a general methodology which applies to the new technologies and which can be imparted without reference to specific subject content? Certainly training only one or two teachers per school will fail them and the school.

When, in the U.K., the Department of Trade and Industry decided to part-finance a micro system for every secondary school, it insisted on teacher training before the recipient schools received their system. This training amounted to two teachers for two days regardless of school size or of the subject specialism of the teachers. The belief was that this would act as a catalyst. In some cases it worked and in other cases it did not.

The other less definable effect is that of the educational tone in a country. There must be a minimum number of teachers who are thinking about, talking about and working with the new technologies before they get visibility and hence credibility within the educational system. It is difficult to give a precise figure here but it depends to a degree on the activist nature of the persons trained.

The biggest single educational problem ever was that of attempting to achieve universal literacy. An early worker in the field, Frank Laubach, coined the slogan, 'Each one Teach one', the belief being that if every individual who had been initiated into the art of reading would teach one other individual to read then in a very short period of time the whole world would be literate. In terms of mathematical progression this is sound, but human frailty resulting in the breaking of a multiplicity of chains ensured that it did not work. Probably in a school it is essential to have some 10 per cent of the staff interested in and committed to the new technologies before there is a noticeable effect on the rest of the staff and hence the school.

Question 2. Who pays?

Throughout the countries in Europe teachers have different forms of contractual obligations to different employers. In some, they are civil servants; in some they are employed by the local authorities or regional authorities; in some a significant number hire out their services privately. Much public money is expended on the education and training of teachers whatever the system in which they ultimately choose to work. Employers have an expectation to obtain services from those whom they pay, and require to be convinced that further training of teachers is to their advantage. If a teacher is taken away from his or her daily duties of teaching, someone else will have to carry out these duties or else they will go by default. This means additional expense and may even lead to complications with the labour laws. Economists use the deceptively simple phrase, 'opportunity costs'.

Most businessmen would agree that it is essential to maintain and protect one's capital. In education the up-to-date knowledge of the teacher is the capital which has to be maintained. One possible solution is for every country to have a central fund which can be drawn upon by those who are the employers of teachers for agreed in-service courses. Such a scheme would help to even out the imbalance which comes from comparisons with urban provision and provision for teachers working in sparsely populated areas.

Question 3. Who trains the teachers?

If teaching is a profession is there an onus on teachers to train themselves? There is an expectation that doctors or lawyers will familiarise themselves with new drugs and with new laws. They may do this at seminars but are much more likely to do it in the first case by reading literature provided by the drug company and in the second case by reading the actual law and perhaps a critique of such by a notable luminary in the profession. If then teaching is a profession should it expect of its practitioners that they keep themselves up-to-date in similar fashion to that of other prefessions? In Ontario this is the expectation but teaching salaries there are comparable to that of other professions. Not so in Britain.

Another aspect of the problem is that where there are new ideas, new techniques and new equipment it may be impossible for the teacher to provide the hardware to learn from it. At one extreme it may be reasonable to expect the teacher to provide a pencil but at the other extreme it is unreasonable to expect him or her to provide a microcomputer system and perhaps interactive video. Some teachers may choose to purchase such equipment for themselves but in most countries the taxation laws are such that they cannot do as is done by professionals in other spheres, and claim allowances against this expenditure.

If we move from the concept of the teacher keeping himself or herself up-to-date to that of group learning under a tutor, the question arises with new technologies of who trains the tutor. Thus courses on the training of trainers are popular. The trainer must master the applications of the new technology before being able to impart it. There then becomes the problem of the credibility of the trainers. It is a common occurrence to criticise lecturers and tutors in colleges of education and in institutes of education on the grounds that they have been away from teaching for so long that they are out of touch and/or out of date. Trainers of trainers must pilot their work in schools on students or they will fail to appreciate the problems which will affect the learner. Thus they need access to educational institutions.

At one time this was less of a problem when a university was a community of scholars which tackled problems in groups and reached solutions predominantly by discussion. There is a shortage of highly skilled trainers and the days of the sabbatical for the professions have gone. There are enough individuals who can explain the technology of hardware but there are not enough individuals who can show how to use this hardware in a different way in teaching. All too often we find the microcomputer being used to teach in a more complicated fashion something which has been and could continue to be taught more simply. In other words, the potential of the microcomputer is not being developed sufficiently for different methods of learning and there are few people working along these lines.

Question 4. What should be taught?

At one level agreement is reached by saying that we must teach 'awareness' of the new technologies. For some this means a philosophical discourse on how society will change because of these new technologies. For others it means learning keyboard skills in order to enter material into a central processor. 'Awareness' may mean acquiring a micro system because it seems the appropriate action to take and then wondering what to do with it. Another argument is about programming. It is fashionable to have contempt for the language Basic. One report in the U.K. (Alvey) said that anyone exposed to Basic at an early age would be damaged for life. There are others who claim that author languages are adequate and have the great advantage that they are easy to learn. They have the great disadvantage that they demand much more memory in the microcomputer. Most machines in use in schools have 32K or at most 64K of memory. Many author languages have shown great initial promise but have failed to fulfil that promise. The biggest single weakness of an author language is that it reflects the teaching methods of today, locks the teaching into that and is inflexible for future development in methodology. Is it reasonable to expect that most teachers will ever become programmers? It is probably appropriate to ensure that all teachers know what a program is and how the central processor handles material presented to it. This is rather different from knowing how a computer works, i.e. the electronics factor. How much elementary maintenance should be taught? There are still many trivial things which can go wrong. This can be disastrous in a school and there is a minimal level of knowledge required so that the teacher can handle the microcomputer effectively and with confidence. Another area of controversy is subject content. Initially the belief was that mathematics and science were the major subjects for computing. Subsequently business studies was added, then geography and now most subjects see appropriate applications for microcomputers. The final area which should have a place in the syllabus is methodologies of learning related to all the new technologies. Paradoxically these methodologies are in themselves a new technology and this is the area where least work has been done.

Question 5. How is the in-service training to be conducted?

We know that it is very expensive to bring teachers together for courses as someone has to continue their work in school. There are distinct advantages in groups learning together and peer culture has been shown to be very effective. There is also the problem of the nature of the group. Any course must have aims and these tend to become rationalisations of practice rather than the basis for a critique. The 'means to end' model in teaching is incomplete because it omits values and education is about values. (Values are implicit in the skills of the tutor, the cultural beliefs of the particular community and in the methods of passing them on to the next generation.) When training groups of teachers in the new technologies the 'group mind' tends to harden convictions and may isolate the individual who wishes to consider other 'methods'.

The cost of the new technologies is such that, as stated above, it is improbable that individuals will be able to afford the resources, and therefore collections of equipment will be needed to enable teachers to practise specific processes. A way to avoid the expense of bringing together large groups of teachers is to use Distance Learning techniques. The Open University and the

Open Tech have gained considerable expertise in this type of learning, even in science subjects where there is a practical component, by providing simple kits. It can only be an effective teaching medium, however, if it is part of a total package with self-instructional material and a back-up system of tutorial help.

Germany is credited rightly or wrongly with having invented the lecture system. It has the advantage of being cheap but there is no guarantee that the students assimilate the information, and are able to apply it. The advent of cheap printing made the dictated note lecture unnecessary and the lecture developed into a semi-dramatic performance. Subsequently other methods such as tutorials and seminars were used. There is the belief that in those groups discussion will lead to consensus.

Probably what the teacher requires more than anything else with the new technologies is enough knowledge to give him or her the confidence to use them in the classroom without being at risk from the pupils. It is commonly held that the pupils today know more about new technologies than the teachers. There is very little evidence for this contention. A few pupils are extremely able and likely to be ahead of the teacher but the vast majority of pupils are not in this category. This has always been the case in any subject and is not peculiar to the new technologies. The teacher must avoid that degree of ego-involvement which will lead to inevitable confrontation.

Probably the best way to run courses of this type is to have some initial training followed by practical workshops at which the teachers can carry out a task related to their own perception of their needs. Once they have reached a minimal level of proficiency in this they can return to their own institutions and carry out further tasks of their own choosing, again related to their own circumstances. Subsequently at a later date they can return to the institution where they had their in-service training and jointly have critiques of the way in which their tasks have been carried out. All this is very time-consuming and inconvenient for administrators of education. It is the most effective way of running in-service courses and is in the John Dewey tradition of 'Democracy and Education' that the student (teacher) must get the education for himself or herself.

The last issue under the 'how' question is the methodology of the course itself. Most teachers model their work on what they have seen or what they have been exposed to in their own learning. Thus if we are going to have efficient methodologies for the new technologies these have to be used in the in-service training. We can all give nightmare accounts of disasters which came from having an expectation of equipment provided in a foreign setting which did not materialise. The moral becomes that of using one's own equipment. Examples are all too common of even a simple piece of teaching apparatus such as the overhead projector being used in a most inefficient way. What shall we do when we try to come to terms with the great potential of the video disk in our information society?

Part II: Issues

4 Nonprint media: a blessing or a curse for reading?

Marian J. Tonjes

Picture if you will the following scenario from Bill Hoest's cartoon. We see a father happily and proudly reading aloud his son's school report card while the lad stands proudly by with a beaming smile. Here is what the report said, 'Programs rapidly, inputs easily, communicates forcefully, and relates well to peer group.' The father says, '*Splendid* son! You can *always* learn to read and write!' (Hoest, 1982). When I saw that cartoon I reacted stongly to it for I, like many educators, had found computers particularly to be an alien form of instruction and I balked at getting too involved. But here was the dilemma – I really needed to overcome my negative feelings, in order to present a fair picture to my students and of course to keep current. I decided to jump in with both feet, read everything I could lay my hands on from the last three years about nonprint media and reading and then boil it all down to a concise list of pitfalls and potentials.

Nonprint media is defined for the purpose of this paper as including microcomputers, television, film, videotext, teletext and tapes as means of conveying information. This is in contrast to the print media of book, magazine, newspaper or pamphlet.

Pitfalls and potentials

Let us look first at some pitfalls and then at some potentials of nonprint media and reading, especially focusing on microcomputers with a brief mention later of television, teletext, videotext and artificial intelligence.

Pitfall 1: sexism

As a woman speaking in this area, and perhaps fitting the stereotype, I want to mention a problem that exists in the U.S.A. and perhaps to a degree in other places – and that is equal time for females in access and use of computers. In a recent article (Kolata, 1984) a strong case was made for the fact that barriers between women and computers are generally social, not intellectual. In California, for example, surveys show that the gap in computer skills between boys and girls starts in primary years and grows through secondary school. At the University of California at Berkeley, social scientists recently found that boys in California outnumber girls by 25 per cent in having microcomputers in their home. Another study by the California Department of Education showed 63 per cent *male* enrolment in computer classes, and a nationwide poll of 17-year-olds showed nearly twice as many boys as girls taking computer programming courses. Stanford University surveyed computer camps and found that *three times* as many boys attended them. The situation persists at the college level too.

One reason for these differences may well have to do with the types of software developed (mostly by men), and the video games that have been the rage in the U.S.A. until very recently. The 'arcade game' mentality of bombing, killing and rape naturally repels most girls. Advertisements for home computers often feature boys raptly intent on the screen and, if girls are shown at all, they are looking on in awed admiration while the boys operate the computer. Parents reinforce these differences by buying home computer games for their sons, not their daughters, and sending them to computer camps first.

Actually we might consider that some of the very traits thought by many as being feminine traits are particularly suitable for computer specialists – traits such as patience and attention to detail. It doesn't really follow that girls are left behind because of lack of aptitude.

Marcus (1983) discussed the fact that while fewer girls use computers they have less access to them, are less likely to choose to use them, if given a choice, and thus often lose interest. The problem, he believes, stems partly from gender bias and role stereotypes. Recreational software in the United States has rewarded aggression, competitiveness and usually features male-oriented images. Classes teaching computer programming often emphasise maths or science problems rather than the language arts areas of interest to many girls.

In my visits to 30 Somerset, Oxfordshire and London inner city schools in 1984, I took a particular interest in looking for evidence of sexism in primary schools and I did find some.

Pitfall 2: *computer literacy*

Another problem we are all aware of is that of computer literacy. As schools continue to purchase microcomputers, teachers are increasingly concerned about their own computer literacy. Obviously, some type of hands-on in-service is necessary to accomplish this and in a format which alleviates the fear, and does the job efficiently for all. So far in the U.S.A., such training has not been mandated across the board, although many school districts do now conduct extensive sessions for their teachers.

Pitfall 3: *teacher sabotage*

Related to problem 2 (computer literacy) are the personal negative attitudes of teachers forced to deal with an area that they find threatening, or feel inadequate to work with. Clement states that poor attitudes on the part of instructors have actually resulted in covert sabotage of the computer-aided learning process. Teachers may feel they are being forced to change their teaching styles, and may assume they are losing some of their power. If they don't see the computer as just another teaching/learning aid they may think they will eventually be replaced. They must be reassured that teacher judgement will always be needed.

Pitfall 4: alienating effects on students

Like television, computers can be addictive and alienating. The world of electronics has been seen as intangible, hypnotic and isolating. It has been argued (Cole, 1982) that we must ensure that microcomputers do not become the pervasive experience of the growing child. There must be an ample variety of traditional, tactile, verbal, human experiences (like family outings, story telling, reading aloud, constructing things, physical contact sports.) It is vital that these 'are not scheduled out of a child's life by the intoxicating notion that these wondrous machines can replace fundamental experiences'.

Another effect on students, besides addiction, is a purely physical one. Users may develop eye strain from the glare of the screen. There is also a tendency for words to blur around the edges, which is not true with regular books.

Thirdly, diversity of reasoning can be stifled when students must perform tasks correctly according to the computer, before moving on. After all, it is often the reason behind the response that is more important than the 'right' answer.

It has been described how computer-assisted instruction favours those who: (1) have the ability to sit still and concentrate quietly, (2) pay attention to accuracy and details, (3) have an affinity for memorising facts, (4) stick to a task until done, (5) have a preference for working alone, (6) have a manual keyboard dexterity, (7) have an aptitude for learning visually, and (8) have a strong intuitive and diagnostic ability (Hoffman and Waters, 1982; Pritchard, 1982). Pritchard declares that many women are less receptive to computer use only because of their strong sense of socialisation. They prefer working with others, having a human contact.

Pitfall 5: software limitations

Much has been written about this area. We all realise that much of the software to date has been limited or slanted more towards simple word recognition types of activities than towards higher level comprehension. This trivial software is little more than workbook pages transferred to a screen, which can actually be more difficult to read than the book itself.

Pitfall 6: hardware limitations

Although tremendous improvements have occurred recently in the microcomputers themselves, there remain two major problems for schools, and those are both financial. There is still a lack of adequate funding for purchase, wiring and repair, to meet the needs of the school population. In terms of access, in Oxfordshire, every school has one computer, which is fine for the small country school, but what about the school with 300 or more pupils? It is going to take time to be able to afford what we need so that every child has fair access.

In summary, pitfalls of computer mania include possible sexism, computer literacy for teachers, teacher sabotage, alienating effects on students, and limitations of both software and hardware. Larrick (1984) recently asked 'Is high technology taking education down the garden path?' and Naisbitt (1982) says we are starving for knowledge, yet drowning in information. Some see computers as monsters eating up school and library budgets. It has been said that we now have three types of reading: survival reading (or decoding key words), 'high tech' or computer reading on a screen, and finally true reading where readers develop transactions with authors with emotional reactions to what is being read.

Now I move to positive potentials of nonprint media: what is already beneficial in existing software, how computers may enhance thinking, writing and creative learning; how television can motivate reading, uses of teletext and videotext, and potential brain language.

Potential 1: *software benefits*

We must not lose sight of what computers can do for us already in the areas of tutorial/drill on basic skills, helping students in applying principles and problem solving and as management tools for teachers. Structured drill is easily programmed and immediate feedback with opportunity for unlimited practice is easily built in. Examples of two programs going beyond basic skills today are 'S.R.A.' and the 'Bank Street Writer'. We need more like them. The 'Bank Street Writer', for example, instructs learners in the principles of word processing and allows users to apply these principles, using the word processor software.

Potential 2: *enhancing thinking*

Papert (1980) in his excellent paperback book on Logo, waxes ecstatic when he talks about computer potential. He calls it the 'Protheus of Machines' with its essence being its universality and power to stimulate. I believe he should be read by all those who feel negative towards computers in the classroom. He believes that, because it can take a thousand forms and serve a thousand functions, it can appeal to a thousand tastes. Computers, he states, can be carriers of powerful ideas, the seeds of cultural change, challenging current beliefs about who can understand what, and at what age. He believes it is possible to design computers so that learning to communicate with them can be a natural process (like learning French by living in France). Papert further feels that learning to communicate with a computer may change the way other learning takes place. It can be a mathematic-speaking and at the same time an alphabetic-speaking entity. The computer as a writing instrument offers students the chance to become more like advanced professionals in their relationship to their intellectual products and to themselves. This is the opposite of the many aspects of school which Papert believes tend to infantilise the child.

44

Students begin to think about thinking which turns them into epistemologists. They are active builders then of their own intellectual structures, appropriating to their own use materials they find about them. It is possible too, he thinks, that computers may be able to concretise and personalise the formal level of thinking for students at an earlier age than Piaget found. Whether we believe all of this to be possible and desirable or not, it behoves us to consider the potential of computers to affect thinking.

Potential 3: enhancing writing

English and Edwards (1984) describe programming as being similar to writing a theme or term paper. It is necessary first to know the audience, to understand the subject, to limit the topic, to control the purpose, to organise the main ideas, to outline, to write and then to revise. If students can't write in clear, concise English they will simply not be successful programmers. All of this requires precision, logic and orderliness on their part. Programmers have one additional step in writing, that of documenting – assisting in answering questions about how the program functions, how to use it, the previous knowledge required, any special features and pertinent information. In a sense it is like writing an advance organiser for what is to come. Mason, Blanchard and Daniel (1983) state that, since writing instructions and practice appears to be conducive to improved reading achievement, word processors which proofread, edit and print will benefit students, and may replace the eventual need for spelling and handwriting. I still believe we will always need to be able to spell correctly and write legibly.

Potential 4: creative learning

I have always been interested in the creative aspects of teaching and learning. Wray (1983) describes some interesting activities being developed today with computers. One example is logic-based activities where the computer presents a situation to a group of children and they must work out a logical response. The computer reacts according to which responses are selected and then poses new problems for the user. This is of course similar to the 'adventure game' where branching occurs according to choices made. These logic-based activities do call for careful reading and purposeful discussion.

A second kind of creative activity is data-based, where users must perceive and select certain patterns from large amounts of data.

Kuechle (1983), a primary teacher in California, described several well known educational techniques combined with using the computer to strengthen reading and writing skill. The D.R.T.A. (Directed Reading/Thinking Activity) is one which asks students to make predictions, forcing them to make their own inferences about characters, feeling and reactions. The interactive capability of the computer lends itself to making predictions while reading and students get immediate feedback. Kuechle believes that teaching children to program is an even better use of the computer as they learn the importance of following directions, using logical thinking, being precise and patient. The only limits on the novelty of working with the computer are set by the user's own creativity.

Marcus (1983) believes we are in the advantageous position now to explore the computer's potential for developing students' abilities to create and understand fiction, non-fiction, and poetry and also allow students to engage in classroom-based research. New demands on student authors for the computer include being able to create appropriate dialogue and command structures for others who will be reading these activities. Students will need to become information artists, graphic designers and architects of knowledge.

Matsuyamo (1984) described the *Yale Artificial Intelligence Project* which is creating a computer to understand a story with several levels of understanding, depending on background knowledge, from event characterisation, event connection, contextual understanding, to intentional and global understanding.

Television and motivating reading

In terms of television it is interesting to note that from a summary of television studies Neuman (1980) found no clear correlation between television viewing and reading achievement. In contrast to this, however, Telfer and Kann (1984) found that students who spent more time with media (television, radio, tapes and records) tended to have lower reading achievement scores. More disturbing was the finding that reading for enjoyment declined with age from fourth year students to eleventh year (Neuman and Prowda, 1982). However, as Shoup (1984) declared, television networks really do want their audiences to know that there is a positive natural link between books and television. Columbia Broadcasting System with the Library of Congress developed a 'Read More About It' programme to 'marry TV with the book'. After these programmes are aired, one of the stars appears on camera to recommend several books for added information.

Instructional television can be an effective teaching tool but a key is in learning to extend the viewing experience by using related materials. I believe from what I have witnessed in British schools that, on the whole, better use is made of instructional television than in the United States.

I think it is important for those still fearful of the media's effect to realise that communication researchers have noted that, when first introduced, television displaced radio, magazines and newspapers. After a period of adjustment, each medium continued to thrive even though it sometimes fulfilled a slightly different function than before. Radio turned to music, magazines to special interest audiences and newspapers expanded to soft features on lifestyles, home and entertainment.

Uses of teletext and videotext

Neuman (1984) in describing teletext and videotext (other nonprint media) stated that they too will simply become resources along with other existing ones.

Teletext transmits text and graphic displays on the television set in the unused portion of the television transmission. Using a decoder the viewer selects from the index page the information or service needed. The page remains in view until the user flips to another page (or back to regular television). Users can select or freeze pages, which are continuously updated. Problems to date with using teletext include: (1) a small data base, therefore providing only general information with popular appeal, (2) a one-way system, so the user cannot interact with it, and (3) too long access time. However it is a 'no frills' version of electronic publishing.

Videotext, on the other hand, is a two-way interactive system, connected by telephone line or a two-way cable, enabling the user to access vast amounts of text and graphic information on a screen. The user talks back to the program via a keyboard similar to a typewriter. The major problem to date is the matter of equipment costs, which are still high. On the other hand, special materials can be developed for a small diverse group such as non-traditional students. Video-text is being tried out in the United States today with such services as teleshopping and telebanking.

Potential brain language

There is a fascinating new area dealing with artificial intelligence and neuroscience. Fortier (1983) talks about reading in the future in terms of brain language or how to read without the eyes. He states the symbiosis of people and computers is beginning to help scientists understand the brain's cognitive functions. Fortier believes that, in the way that computers understand machine language only, humans may develop brain language where words are replaced by electrical signals, encoded and decoded automatically by the brain. This brain language would govern all language activities. Words would be replaced by electrical signals. Some say by 2001 the written word will no longer be our primary means of communicating information.

Implications

What are some implications of nonprint media for reading? What might we, as reading educators, do to contribute? To start off we might:

(1)   Begin to investigate with our colleagues further applications for higher level comprehension.
(2)   Help others to distinguish between using computers for teaching and using them for management tools for the classroom.
(3)   Discriminate between features that contribute to or are superfluous to learning to read.
(4)   And finally, persuade the business world to provide more resources through more grants and gifts.

If we believe John Naisbitt, high technology is here to stay, like it or not, as we move from an industrial society to an information society, with 'high tech' hopefully balanced with 'high touch', or affective, concerns. In reading we must move with the times, and utilise these technological tools to enhance, not inhibit, voluntary successful reading.

Nonprint media and reading: a blessing or a curse? I leave it to you to decide.

References

COLE, P. (1982) *Practical Applications of Research* (Newsletter of Phi Delta Kappa's Center on Evaluation, Development and Research, Bloomington, Ind.), 4(4).

DREYFUS, H. L. (1972) *What Computers Can't Do: A Critique of Artificial Reason*. New York: Harper & Row.

ENGLISH, R. and EDWARDS, G. (1984) 'Programming as a writing activity'. *The Computing Teacher*, 11(6), pp. 46–7.

FORTIER, G. (1983) 'Reading in the future. The brain language, or how to read without the eyes'. *Journal of Reading*, 27(2), pp.164–8.

HOEST, B. (1982) 'Laugh Parade'. *Parade*, 21, 22 March.

HOFFMAN, J. L. and WATERS, K. (1982) 'Some effects of student personality on success with computer-assisted instructions'. *Educational Technology*, 20, 21.

KOLATA, G. (1984) 'Equal time for women'. *Discover*, 5(1), pp.24–31.

KUECHLE, N. (1983) 'Reading, writing and programming'. *Computers, Reading and Language Arts*, 2, pp.7–10.

LARRICK, N. (1984) 'Beyond the Big Apple', paper presented at the International Reading Associations National Convention in Atlanta, Georgia.

MARCUS, S. (1983) 'Sexism and CAI'. *Computers, Reading and Language Arts*, 2(6), p.10.

MASON, G. E., BLANCHARD, J. S. and DANIEL, D. B. (1983) *Computer Applications in Reading* (2nd edn.). International Reading Association.

MATSUYAMO, U. (1984) paper presented at the W.O.R.D. Reading Research Conference, Bellevue, Wash., 9 March.

NAISBITT, J. (1982) *Megatrends*. New York: Warner.

NEUMAN, S. B. (1980) 'Television: its effects on reading and school achievement'. *The Reading Teacher*, 33(7), pp.801–5.

NEUMAN, S. B. (1984) 'Teletext/videotext: the future of the print media.' *Journal of Reading*, 27(4), pp.340–44.

NEUMAN, S. B. and PROWDA, P. (1982) 'Television viewing and reading achievement'. *Journal of Reading*, 25(7), pp.666–71.

PAPERT, S. (1980) *Mindstorms: Children, Computers, and Powerful Ideas*. New York: Basic Books.

PRITCHARD, W. J., Jnr. (1982) 'Instructional computing in 2001: a scenario'. *Phi Delta Kappa*, pp.322–5.

SHOUP, B. (1984) 'Television: friend, not foe to the teacher'. *Journal of Reading*, 27(7), pp.629–31.

TELFER, R. J. and KANN, R. S. (1984) 'Reading achievement, free reading, watching and listening to music'. *Journal of Reading*, 27(6), pp.636,539.

WRAY, D. (1983) 'Computer-assisted learning in language and reading'. *Reading*, 17(1), pp.31–5.

5   Before a byte, the L.I.T.E. approach to literacy

Joyce M. Morris

In the United Kingdom it would seem that computer-assisted learning (C.A.L.) and computer-assisted instruction (C.A.I.) are here to stay. However, it would be foolhardy to predict how educationally significant C.A.L. and C.A.I. will be specifically as a contribution to universal literacy in English and especially to the early stages of literacy acquisition.

Much depends on whether computer programmers can meet the challenge of devising programs which have sound didactic objectives, and yet are sufficiently stimulating to captivate today's children accustomed, as many of them are, to exciting computer games with little or no educational content. This is a tall order and reminiscent of that experienced with another technology when, in 1964, the British Broadcasting Corporation pioneered the teaching of reading on television, and producers working with the writer as consultant had to come to terms with competition from 'showbiz-type' children's programmes, including the subsequent development and importation of series such as 'Sesame Street' from the U.S.A.

Even more so, it is reasonable to suppose that the educational significance of C.A.L. and C.A.I. will depend on the same school variables for literacy acquisition which were highlighted in a summary of research findings at the first U.K.R.A. annual conference (Morris, 1966). These variables have largely decided the fate of other innovations such as the initial teaching alphabet, also discussed at the inaugural conference (Downing, 1966), of which the most crucial is the supply of teachers with the requisite attitudes, specialised knowledge and classroom expertise. Moreover, as subsequent conference contributions have emphasised in such papers as 'You can't teach what you don't know' (Morris, 1973), it is the knowledge of teachers which is of fundamental importance.

The prime need for linguistics-informed teachers

Accordingly, at this twenty-first anniversary Conference when reading and the new technologies is a central concern, it would seem appropriate to draw attention once again to the prime need for knowledgeable teachers who, above all, are 'Linguistics-informed'. In consequence, amongst other things, they can judge whether computer reading (and spelling) programs are soundly based on 'linguistically-defensible' information from the scientific study of language. After all, it would be ludicrous to enter the new microcomputer era in education encumbered by the kind of linguistic folklore which, regrettably, remains in evidence both in current professional literature and in print resources for classroom use. It would also be ludicrous to train teachers in the 'bytes' etc., of computer language and use before making sure, through a 'Linguistics In Teacher Education' (L.I.T.E.) approach to literacy, that they have sufficient explicit knowledge about the nature of English in spoken and written form for their respective tasks, including the development of computer literacy. In short, as its title indicates, this paper is concerned with priorities. More precisely, it is concerned with summarising, in the limited space available, a few of the findings from a recent research project which puts the spotlight on a basic problem for teacher-trainers responsible for pre-service literacy courses. (More details will be given elsewhere, and it is planned to publish a full report in 1986 which will include results from comparative studies involving other researchers.)

Research rationale and questionnaire

Briefly, the rationale of the research is that the 'language awareness' which student teachers will eventually need to promote literacy in schools (computer-assisted and/or otherwise) should be developed on the same 'starter' principles which govern sound classroom practice. In other words, the pre-service training of literacy teachers should begin where students are in terms of their linguistic knowledge, etc., just as classroom practice for literacy acquisition should begin where children are.

With this in mind, the writer designed a 'Starter Quiz' to tap aspects of a student's basic knowledge of the phonological and visible systems of English at the beginning of his/her course of study. Permission was then sought and given for the questionnaire to be administered, in October 1983, by eight tutors at the largest teacher-training establishment in Britain. However, at the request of one of the tutors, some of the original questions and tasks were first amended to include 'softeners' like 'Can you?' and 'Please'. This was because it was felt that students would be put off by the formal language normally used in professionally-designed questionnaires. Predictably, a few students simply replied 'Yes' or 'No', as the case may be, to questions beginning with 'Can you?', and this naturally swelled the number of 'no attempt' answers.

The undergraduate sample

At the outset, it was made clear that the 'fresher' students were free to decide whether to co-operate in the research and, as names were not required, anonymity was assured. Overall, the response was good in that 275 undergraduates out of a possible 338 (counting absentees through illness etc.) agreed to be 'quizzed' about their basic linguistic knowledge.

In rounded figures, 94 per cent of the co-operative undergraduate sample is female, 82 per cent under 20 years of age and, for 99 per cent, English is their mother tongue. With one exception (C.S.E. only), all have passed the O-level English examination, and 53 per cent have also gained an A-level pass in English prior to entering college.

Of the 275 undergraduates, 73 per cent are taking the B.Ed. course (13 per cent with main subject English) and training to teach children in the 3 to 13 age range. The rest (27 per cent) are studying educational theory only as part of their B.A. course, and English is the main subject of 3 per cent of them. This means that a total of 16 per cent (all with an A-level English pass) are potential graduates in English and, as such, the only group guaranteed some teaching by a specialist in linguistics.

Some results

Considering the above sample data, it is reasonable to expect that all the undergraduates would respond well to the simple questions and tasks in the Starter Quiz. Alas! This was far from the case as the following selected examples demonstrate.

Question 1

The English writing system is basically alphabetic. Can you say what alphabetic symbols represent?

Response

No answer	26%
Incorrect answer	21%
Sounds	49%
Speech sounds	2%
Phonemes	2%

Question 4b

The fact that there are many more *vowel sounds* (phonemes) in spoken English than there are *vowel letters* (graphemes) may be a source of difficulty for children learning to read and spell whatever their dialect.

How many vowel sounds do you think there are in the 'standard' English dialect known as Received Pronunciation or R.P. for short?

Response
No answer 32%
Thirty-two different answers ranging from 1–4 vowel sounds (3% of students) to 50–500 vowel sounds (3% of students)
Correct answer (20 vowel sounds) given by only 6% of students

Task 5

In the following words, please ring each letter or combination of letters which you think may represent a distinct sound (phoneme), and put the number of sounds under each word. Example: (th)a(t).

3

fisher   swing   mishap   cough   apple

Response

No attempt	3%
All incorrect	54%
1 correct	21%
2–4 correct	21%
All correct	1%

Question 6a

What is the name given to English *words* which sound the same but have a different spelling and meaning?

Response

No answer	79%
Incorrect answer	20%
Homonyms ⎫ Homophones ⎭	1%

Task 8c

Please give first the *comparative* form and then the *superlative* form beside each of the adjectives below.

fat	fine	sly	bad	tall
good	rough	merry	beautiful	curious

Response

No attempt	21%
All incorrect	5%
Some errors	56%
All correct	18%

A total of 523 errors were made, not counting 'curiouser' with deference to Lewis Carroll. Of the selected errors below, 32 examples were contributed by students with A-level English passes reading English for a degree.

bad	– badder, naughty, good.
	– baddest, badest, worsest.
good	– gooder, well, well-behaved.
	– goodest, bad.
merry	– merryer, sad, happy.
	– merryest, merryiest, sad.
beautiful	– beautifuller, pretty, ugly.
	– beautifullest, loveliest.

Task 9c

In the following sentences, please put a stress mark before the syllable which has primary 'strong' stress in the words *conduct, produce, content, project, console*.

1.   The conduct of the conductor was strange when he began to conduct.
2.   In the market, the farmer began to produce his produce.
3.   She was content with the content of her latest book.
4.   Their project was to project new ideas on computers.
5.   The sound from the console did not console her.

Response

No attempt	14%
All incorrect	17%
Some errors	34%
All correct	35%

Question 10a

Linguistics is the systematic study of language in spoken and written form. Only a tiny fraction of basic linguistic knowledge *of* and *about* English is tapped in this quiz;

How useful would this kind of knowledge have been to you in your English language studies at school?

Please tick one of the boxes below.

☐ not useful   ☐ fairly useful   ☐ useful   ☐ very useful

Response

No answer	10%
Not useful	12%
Fairly useful	28%
Useful	29%
Very useful	21%

Task 10b

Explain briefly the reason(s) for your answer to the previous question.

Response

Varied and, in a few cases, very revealing and thought-provoking.

Comments on the results

Even from the few results given above, it is obvious that many of the undergraduates, including some reading English for a degree, were starting their college courses without the very basic knowledge of English which they will need to follow these courses successfully. They are lacking knowledge, indeed, which their tutors should be able to take for granted, in view of the students' A-level or O-level qualifications.

Some students were well aware of their deficiencies and drew attention to them by adding remarks to their returned questionnaires such as 'I can't spell', and 'I don't understand the meaning of comparative and superlative forms'. (The errors recorded for Task 8c above are indicative of the general lack of terminology to discuss language.) Others suggested that their ignorance could be attributed to the fact that they had studied English Literature and not English Language at school. But this made it all the more difficult to understand why, in answer to Question 6a, instead of the correct word 'homophones', they offered words such as 'similes' and 'metaphors', the meaning of which is surely necessary for the study of English literature in schools.

Sadly, about 12 per cent of the students who manifested crass ignorance about their own language, and who also responded to both Question 10a and Task 10b, did not seem to think that their linguistic ignorance mattered. Perhaps this is understandable because it had not prevented them from getting A- and/or O-level qualifications. However, as a few of them pointed out, they had learned to read (if not to spell) with comparatively little difficulty.

It is to be hoped that college tutors will manage to persuade those students that, especially if they are to be teachers of literacy, they cannot work successfully in the classroom without explicit linguistic knowledge. Meanwhile, the majority positive response to Question 10a is encouraging to those who, in increasing numbers, are promoting the idea of 'language awareness' courses in schools and, in a few instances, have already published valuable classroom resources such as the *Awareness of Language Series* edited by Eric Hawkins (1984).

The response to Question 10a and the results of the Starter Quiz project in general also support the work of the Committee for Linguistics in Education on which the writer represents UKRA. This joint committee of the Linguistics Association of Great Britain (L.A.G.B.) and the British Association for Applied Linguistics (B.A.A.L.) has recently produced a working paper called *Guidelines for Evaluating School Instruction about Language* (C.L.I.E., 1984), which focuses attention on the inadequate linguistic knowledge of school leavers. These even include first-year university students who have chosen to specialise in the study of language. For example, university teachers of linguistics and applied linguistics report that very many of their 'fresher' students 'find it hard to distinguish between a word's pronunciation and its spelling', and 'they know virtually nothing about the structure of their own language'. Moreover 'they have very little knowledge of terminology of discussing matters of style and other kinds of variation within their own language.' Accordingly, the C.L.I.E. working paper (No. 4) provides a useful basis for the consideration of all pertinent matters concerned with removing the 'unnecessary' linguistic ignorance of school leavers.

Final word

Clearly, if future research supports the main findings of the Starter Quiz project, and there are grounds for believing it will, the powers-that-be may be persuaded that the advent of microcomputers in schools and colleges is of secondary importance to the need for linguistics in teacher education and courses on 'language awareness' in schools.

Fourteen years ago, with others, the writer emphasised this need in evidence to the House of Commons Select Committee on Education and Science (Morris, 1970). But, for various reasons, the educational climate was not ripe for the necessary action to be taken. Now, as indicated above, the need is becoming so much more widely acknowledged that, if linguistics-informed programmers were to provide appropriate software, C.A.L. and C.A.I. could become educationally significant in this important area and, thereby, make a valuable contribution to the goal of universal literacy in the United Kingdom.

References

C.L.I.E. (1984) *Guidelines for Evaluating School Instruction about Language*. Working Paper No. 4. B.A.A.L./L.A.G.B. Committee for Linguistics in Education. (Available for a first class stamp and an S.A.E. from Dick Hudson, Department of Phonetics and Linguistics, University College, Gower Street, London WC1 6BT.)

DOWNING, J. A. (1966). 'The initial teaching alphabet', in J. A. Downing (ed) *The First International Reading Symposium*. London: Cassell.

HAWKINS, E. (1984) *Awareness of Language Series*. Cambridge: Cambridge Educational.

MORRIS, J. M. (1966) 'How far can reading backwardness be attributed to school conditions?', in J. A. Downing (ed) *The First International Reading Symposium*. London: Cassell.

MORRIS, J. M. (1970) 'Published minutes of evidence on reading education taken before the House of Commons Select Committee on Education and Science', in *Teacher Training: Teaching of Reading*. London: H.M.S.O.

MORRIS, J. M. (1973) 'You can't teach what you don't know', in M. Clark and A. Milne (eds) *Reading and Related Skills*. London: Ward Lock Educational.

6   The microcomputer in home and school

Tony Obrist

> There'll be enough good software in homes in five years' time to make truancy educationally worthwhile. (Bailey, 1984)

> Teaching is a complex specialist skill. Every aspect of reading development requires specialist application. Satisfactory progress can be achieved only by excellent teachers. I should also refuse major surgery from a hospital porter. (quoted by Stierer, 1984)

These two quotations represent differing views on learning and teaching. We shall start by considering the numbers and types of microcomputers in homes and schools.

There are now over 2,000,000 home computers in Britain. Two surveys referred to in June 1984 and carried out by Audits of Great Britain and The Valley Organisation, produce roughly the same total of two-and-a-quarter million domestic micros.

The largest proportion of home computers are Sinclair Spectrums. At 36 per cent, this means getting on for 800,000 Spectrums. Another 7 per cent are Sinclair ZX81s. Commodore computers, the successors to the P.E.T., account for perhaps 25 per cent, say 550,000. Acorn–B.B.C. computers are a depressingly low 10 per cent – perhaps 220,000 – in spite of the enormous influence of the B.B.C. and a wide adoption of the B.B.C. micro in the primary field by education authorities.

Others – Dragon, Lynx, Atari, Texas and several others – account for perhaps under 20 per cent. These are the also-rans that have not yet made the grade into the mass market or perhaps have fallen by the wayside.

If we now look at the primary school situation, what do we find? There are about 27,000 primary schools. Micros have arrived, or are in the process of arriving, in the majority of these, so that we might assume a total of 27,000 micros in primary schools since some schools have more than one micro and others have none. The main point at issue is the difference between $2 \cdot 25$ million and 27,000. Even if the secondary schools with their average of seven micros per school are included, there will be little effect on the size of the difference.

Coming back to the primary school, what sort of micros have been installed? Figures are subject to some uncertainty, with considerable regional variation; nevertheless the primary school percentages are generally accepted as being about:

B.B.C.	80%
R.M.L.	15%
Spectrum	5%

Applying these percentages to the figure of 27,000 micros in primary schools gives the following table:

	School	Home
B.B.C.	21,600	220,000
R.M.L.	4,050	a few?
Spectrum	1,350	800,000
ZX81	a few	160,000
Commodore	a few	550,000
Other	a few?	520,000
	27,000	2,250,000

The difference between homes and schools is enormous. Even if we extrapolate into the future there is no comfort to be gained. The M.E.P. scheme which has provided 50 per cent of finance for primary school micros is coming to an end. Some local authorities have provided more generous support for equipment; some such as the Inner London Education Authority have even gone as far as financing the total purchase for every school of an R.M.L. micro with disk drive and monitor (without the school having to provide 50 per cent of the cost). Certain authorities are also going on to provide printers and monitors. But overall the support given so far seems unlikely to continue, given the financial and perhaps political situation. At the same time the forecast sales of micros into the domestic market during 1984 are well in excess of a further million.

Thus there is a substantial discrepancy in numbers of micros. The purchase of home micros seem set to continue at an enormous pace while schools' purchases will trickle on, and then only if we are lucky and the schools go all out to get parental support. No way does the disparity look like diminishing.

A few primary schools are pressing on rapidly with the introduction of the micro across the curriculum, but in the majority it is as yet a question of consolidation or else the slow process of initial introduction. Some schools seem to have made little progress over the last 12 months despite the support or clamour of the parents and it is to be hoped that this is not going to prove at all a widespread pattern.

There is a temptation in some areas to use the micro for skill and drill programs, although in Britain there is, fortunately, a vocal teachers' lobby protesting against this and against using the micro as an easy way of testing children. Clearly in spite of all the talk about data bases and the appearance of Logo, there is a temptation in some areas to employ the micro for mechanising the existing system, however dangerous this might be in the long run.

David Chandler (1984) places this argument in context as follows:

Fortunately the computer was not designed as a piece of 'educational technology' for schools: it was designed far more broadly as a tool for extending our intellectual capabilities. The issue of whether or not to introduce

57

computers into schools is, however, leading some to think again about the adequacy of curricula. Perhaps one of the most valuable effects of the appearance of microcomputers in schools has been to generate discussion about such matters as the nature of learning, children as thinkers, our concepts of 'childhood', issues of control and the future of educational institutions.

Considering the situation in education we may well ask, 'What is being done with micros in the home?' The quick answer is that whatever may have been the reason for purchasing the micro in the first instance, the overwhelming use of micros in the home is to play arcade games of the 'Space Invader' type. These have been shown to encourage speed of response, good co-ordination and extension of the concentration span. They might also develop excessively competitive instincts and give rein to the urge to destroy. Some may also fear that they will encourage children to regard micros as war-oriented devices and that, as has proved to be the case, they can discourage girls from using micros at all.

The other current major use of the home micro seems to be for programming and, at the present time, this means programming in Basic. While I would be one of the last people to advocate that teachers should become involved in learning about Basic and I have argued against any requirement for teachers or children to learn Basic in the primary school, I would not want to underrate the value for today's primary child of learning Basic at home. The arguments for learning Basic, however, are rather like those which used to be advanced for learning Latin – that is, that it is a good discipline for the mind, fun for those who like it, but likely to be of very little practical value. (It is also capable of putting many children off the subject for life.)

The reason for suggesting that Basic is not a desirable subject in school is that the rate of technical development in the field of computers in general is truly terrifying. By the time the majority of present primary children reach employment age Basic will, in all probability, have been superseded by a much improved, higher level language.

Surprisingly perhaps, in view of these strictures, I would want to suggest that some programming in Basic for the proportion of primary age children who can cope with it can be distinctly advantageous from the point of view of reading, as long as neither parents nor teachers anticipate that any but a small minority of children will turn into successful programmers using this language.

The virtues of programming in Basic relate to the systems analysis work which should be done before starting a program, i.e. deciding step by step precisely what it is you want to do. Another virtue is after that, in writing the program: the absolute total accuracy required in keying in the program. Every letter must be totally correct. Every punctuation mark (since these are part of the Basic instructions) must be correct. And every space must be correct. In attaining this the rewards for the child can be considerable. As someone said to me recently, 'I still can remember the sudden sense of power from getting the computer to do what I wanted for the first time.'

58

But only a small proportion of children will be able to do more than simple programming in Basic. The language does not lend itself to breaking down tasks to small isolatable routines and, as a result, the inevitable debugging (which can be a rewarding process with the right sort of language) becomes a long and frustrating affair. Children can be totally put off programming by attempting Basic and all the advantages of exploring a computer environment will be lost. As a result, they go back to arcade games.

I have said nothing up to this point about Logo and for the very good reason that I have only heard of its being used in the home. But I shall return to this later.

Another area of use in the home is what we could call classical games. Children are using micros for games ranging from noughts and crosses through to draughts and chess. But these users are hardly the average children – they are much more probably the ones with the type of mind which will overcome the problems of programming in Basic! Other games which seem to be very successful are word games such as Scrabble and, for those who have a mind to it, the micro will act as a bridge tutor. For simpler minds a program playing Snap is available, but this would appear to be of limited value compared to the real thing.

When you ask parents why they bought a micro, they often reply that it was to aid their children's education and in some cases you find that a couple of educational programs have been purchased, but that they are used very little. The children are described as being bored with them after a short time, as if they had grown out of them, like clothes. Parents think what they want is a lending library for software. Probably they are thinking along the same lines as books – the number of books purchased is limited while book borrowing from libraries is substantial.

There is another area where home computers are being used which is of particular interest because these types of programs, or indeed the same programs, running on the same micros, may also be found in some primary schools. The area covers simulations and adventure games. Perhaps the best known program in this context is 'The Hobbit'. Children read the book first, and then go to the micro to follow through the story. Each time they play the response appears to be different, depending on such things as the decisions taken by the players and the speed and duration of play. The computer understands the English sentences which are keyed in by the players. It may respond, 'I do not understand the word ....' at which point an alternative has to be tried. This is not for children in isolation but for small groups to discuss, plan and play and the program may go on for hours or even days. When it is time to stop, dump the situation onto tape and let another group have a go.

Is this learning at home or learning in school – and does it really matter?

Adventure games may also be role playing, such as 'Dungeons and Dragons', or problem solving such as 'Castle of Dreams' – 'A brain teasing Exploration for 11 year olds and above. Pit your wits against the wicked Magician Klingsor and save the world from his evil' (Widgit, 1984). It is hardly great literature but the kids love it and will play it over and over again.

Each time you play the game is different. Analysis and logical thought. Home or school?

There are further extensions of these types of programs. In one situation – this time in a school – the children were writing their own adventure programs. This is not programming in the sense of Basic but something much more akin to the very high level language suggested earlier as the norm for the future. The children were using a program called 'The Quill' which enabled them, within limits, to devise an adventure involving their own characters and their own locations. This program is a form of authoring program. How exciting for children to locate their adventure game in the next town or in the next school and then try their own adventures out on their peers. Excitingly this type of authoring program can be used by professionals as well as children. 'As Gilsoft and others are showing, use of The Quill doesn't automatically produce a series of conveyor-belt adventures, they can be as bad or as good as the author's imagination allows and "Devil's Island" would be good no matter how it was written' (Anon, 1984).

This form of programming leads us to Logo, almost unknown in the home and just coming into the schools. Two quotations from the advertising for new versions of Logo set this in context.

LOGO is a powerful programming language based on logic. It's very easy to learn, so it's proved highly successful in schools. LOGO puts you in command of a graphic 'turtle' (a moving on-screen cursor). Each program instruction you make has a direct effect on the turtle. You can change its position, alter the direction it points in, and then use it to create complex shapes, images or designs. With LOGO you've the means to develop very imaginative ideas – and see the results immediately.

The Sinclair version of LOGO comes with two comprehensive manuals. It features turtle graphics, colour and sound and has a full list of processing capabilities. It's also Microdrive-compatible and can control a mechanical turtle or robot. (Sinclair Research Ltd., 1984)

LCSI LOGO for the BBC offers true animation, with programmable sprites, allowing planes to fly, turtles to swim, rabbits to hop and dragons to breathe smoke all over the screen. Written in assembly language it's lightning fast. (Logotron Ltd., 1984)

Logo clearly has its place in the home as well as in the school and with these new, powerful versions becoming available it is likely to spread rapidly in both areas.

Lastly, we could touch on the use of micros for early learning. Here we only have space to list a range of areas covered:

letter recognition
word recognition
shape sorting
simple adding and subtracting
basic memory training.

These are the areas of initial learning, some part of which already takes place in both home and school. They are areas where the micro is now beginning to show its uses. With more than two million micros in the home, with more effective software and more effective technology coming along, there is a challenge to be faced both by teachers and by parents. Shall we arrive at a point where we can truly say that we are no longer addressing an audience specifically of teachers or parents as such, but only a group of people concerned with helping children to embark on the adventure of learning?

References

ANON (1984) Review in *Which Micro?*, 8(84), p.84.
BAILEY, W. (1984) *Microscope*, 12(15).
CHANDLER, D. (1984) *Young Learners and the Microcomputer*. Milton Keynes: Open University Press.
LOGOTRON LTD. (1984) *Educational Computing*, 7(84), p.31.
SINCLAIR RESEARCH LTD. (1984) *Educational Computing*, 7(84), p.15.
STIERER, B. (1984) *Times Educational Supplement*, 29 June.
WIDGIT SOFTWARE LTD. (1984) Publicity Material.

7   Monitoring reading for learning in teachers and children

Roger Beard

At a time when there is much discussion and debate throughout the school age range on educational assessment, it becomes clear that little has been done to consider how reading for learning can be assessed. Children use non-fiction books on a selective basis in most primary schools, particularly in what is often called 'topic' or 'project' work. (The two terms will be used here synonymously.) But the ways in which teachers can most effectively monitor such use, *especially as children are engaged in the task itself*, remains a seriously underresearched issue.

Where there has been some progress in this area of the curriculum, it has tended to be limited to a concentration on the issue of *what* is to be monitored, rather than *how*, such as the drawing up of networks of skills (e.g. Merritt *et al.*, 1977) which might be used in criterion-referenced or informal assessments of children's abilities to consult and use non-fiction books efficiently and effectively. There has also been progress in delineating the ways in which children's discussion of 'modified' or 'analysed' texts can be generated in 'Directed Activities Related to Texts' (Lunzer and Gardner, 1984), in which the focus is on the group rather than the individual.

Both these sources of progress are to be welcomed. The teaching profession needs to be critically aware of the skill networks which are an organic part of using books. One of the main implications of the surveys of schools by Her Majesty's Inspectorate (D.E.S., 1978, 1982, 1983) is that reading skills are not being 'extended' to include appropriate book-use skills in ways that we might have expected in the ten years since the Bullock Report (D.E.S., 1975) emphasised the importance of these skills in the curriculum.

Furthermore, the teaching profession needs to recognise the significance of any effective means of generating group work in schools. One of the principal outcomes of the intensive study of 58 junior classrooms in the ORACLE project (Galton *et al.*, 1980) is the finding that the 'physical grouping' of desks and tables rarely leads to the 'psychological grouping' of collaborative learning between children.

As yet, the role of the microcomputer in facilitating reading for learning in schools has scarcely begun to be properly considered. It seems very likely that the microcomputer will provide a new dimension to the 'what' of reading-for-learning, as Golby (1982, p.213) recognises:

If key books could be re-processed into programs which will answer a developing line of inquiry in a child's mind and provide for idiosyncratic styles of learning in individual children, then we would have gone a long way towards rendering the inaccessible book a manageable educational tool.

For a moment, however, this paper will concentrate on the possibilities of the 'how' in monitoring reading-for-learning in schools and the kinds of roles which the microcomputer might play.

In order to examine such possibilities, any theoretical perspectives to be used will need to be linked with the models of skill network and the strategies of promoting group discussion which are presented in the publications mentioned earlier. It is all too easy to fragment the components of classroom behaviour and learning, so that only an artificial, 'de-contextualised' picture is drawn. Two different theoretical perspectives will be brought together here, one concerned with the notion of a 'learning conversation'; the other with the use of writing for 'referential' aims. In the first the microcomputer has already been used in an important facilitative way; in the second its potential has yet to be realised.

In the realisation of this potential, it is important to recognise the value of teacher–pupil relationships in the context of topic work. The microcomputer is likely to be most effectively used in topic work where teacher–pupil relationships are developed which recognise the implications of adopting the individualised learning schedules assumed in the kind of project/topic work being considered here. This means teachers creating a sensitivity to what individual pupils bring to any learning experience and how they structure that experience in their own terms. Thus the teacher intervenes to promote self awareness and to help the learner engage in this structuring process, in a way which can be as much client-centred 'counselling' as teaching. Some of the dimensions of such a non-directive approach and the way in which the microcomputer can be harnessed to it can be illustrated by reference to a research project in a different setting: a study dealing with the evaluation of an in-service course (Beard, 1982). This study has an important link with the challenge of monitoring project work in schools, as it was an attempt to assess the influence of an in-service reading course on teachers, looking particularly at their awareness of the broad area of reading for learning. As the course itself was heavily book-based, the knowledge of teachers on book-use skills and strategies took on an interesting, reflexive importance. But the most significant similarity to be identified is that both settings lend themselves to the use of a 'learning conversation'.

Monitoring children's reading and writing in topic work

The challenging circumstances in which children find themselves in topic work are emphasised by Figure 1, which compares the individualised topic approach with three alternative 'reading contexts' which are discussed in detail in Supramaniam and Beard (1982). The topic demands that the child works on an individualised curriculum at the very time when there are the greatest demands on him or her to take decisions and work systematically.

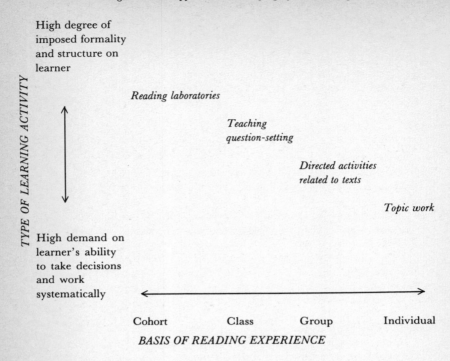

Figure 1: Four approaches to developing reflective reading

High degree of
imposed formality
and structure on
learner

TYPE OF LEARNING ACTIVITY

Reading laboratories

*Teaching
question-setting*

*Directed activities
related to texts*

Topic work

High demand on
learner's ability
to take decisions
and work
systematically

Cohort   Class   Group   Individual

BASIS OF READING EXPERIENCE

Michael Marland (1978, p.371) recognised the major demands that the topic or project can make:

> ... the highest academic accolade is given to somebody who can see a problem that requires investigation, then defines that problem, and can trace the sources of information to help him investigate it; who, having traced the sources, can gut the books to get the relevant data; can then (almost the hardest intellectual feat of all) re-organise that information in the correct sequence and then write it up. Now, if you can do that, Oxford (University) gives you a DPhil. We, in our wisdom, call that 'the project method' and we have used it for the least able and the least well-motivated people in schools. I am not saying we shouldn't do it; all I am saying is that we ought to realise what we have done. I am not denigrating the project system: I am denigrating people like me, who have elevated it to the status of prime teaching method without the concomitant, which is suitable teaching to support it.

It is understandable that this leads to a situation in which the Bullock Committee found that, on the basis of their visits to schools, 'much of the writing done in the name of topic work amounts to no more than copying' (D.E.S., 1975, p.393). The danger of superficiality in topic or project work has been 'sent up' by the author, Jan Mark (1976, pp.32–5) in her award-winning children's novel, *Thunder and Lightnings*. Andrew has moved from London to East Anglia and his new teacher, Miss Beale, is too busy to explain the nature of the project work to him. She sends him over to one of Andrew's new class-mates, Victor, who has some intriguing ideas on the possibilities of project work:

'What are we supposed to be doing?' he asked.

'That rather depends on you', said Miss Beale. 'In General Studies you can choose your own subject and follow it through. You'll be rather behind the others but can start on a project now and work on it through the holidays. That's what most of the others will do, if they haven't finished by next week.'

Andrew found this hard to believe.

'What are you interested in?' asked Miss Beale.

'Motor racing, guinea-pigs', said Andrew.

'Well, either of those would do for a start', said Miss Beale ....

'Miss Beale said you would show me round, to look at the projects', said Andrew.

'Why, do you want to copy one?' asked Victor, lifting a strand of hair and exposing one eye. 'You could copy mine, only someone might recognize it. I've done that three times already.'

'Whatever for?' said Andrew. 'Don't you get tired of it?'

Victor shook his head and his hair.

'That's only once a year. I did that two times at the junior school and now I'm doing that again', he said, 'I do fish, every time. Fish are easy. They're all the same shape.'

'No, they're not', said Andrew.

'They are when I do them', said Victor. He spun his book round, with one finger, to show Andrew the drawings. His fish were not only all the same shape, they were all the same shape as slugs. Underneath each drawing was a printed heading: BRAEM: TENSH: CARP: STIKLBAK: SHARK. It was the only way of telling them apart. The shark and the bream were ident-ical, except that the shark had a row of teeth like tank traps.

'Isn't there a 'c' in stickleback?' said Andrew. Victor looked at his work.

'You're right.' He crossed out both 'k's, substituted 'c's and pushed the book away, the better to study it. 'I got that wrong last year.'

In a small exploratory research project which is being currently planned, some of the 'dynamics' of the reading and writing involved in topic work will be investigated by a group of teachers working co-operatively with researcher-support in the way envisaged by Stenhouse (1975).

To begin with, a sample of children in each class will be studied discreetly by their class teacher to try to establish a base-line of information of their book-use skills. Later in the term, once a curriculum has been developed in which the use of reference books is seen to be part of a natural progression of activity and experience (D.E.S., 1975, p.190), then the children will be monitored by means of a form of the learning conversation described earlier. This is likely to include some investigation of three dimensions of their task involvement: what they have brought to the task in the way of past experience, expectations and purposes; the ways in which they are 'making sense' of what the book has to offer and their awareness of its 'readability'; and, thirdly, the ways in which 'referents' of learning can be negotiated and discussed.

In addition, this exploratory research may throw some light on the nature of the reader–text relationship discussed in Otto and White (1982) and the 'metacognitive' processes in children's reading for learning (Brown, 1980). But it will be important to keep sight of the curriculum and personal context of this reading, factors which are neglected in some reading research reports published in sources from the field of cognitive psychology.

Two additional considerations seem important at this preparatory stage in the research: the potential of the microcomputer in facilitating the individualisation of learning and, secondly, the role of writing in the reading for learning process.

The microcomputer in topic work

At the moment the role of the microcomputer in project work can be seen as falling into three possibilities (Hodges, 1984): firstly, supporting the acquisition of facts and knowledge such as 'Locks' which shows how canal locks operate; secondly, information retrieval such as 'Factfile' which provides children with a means of processing the information which they decide is important in their topic (see for example Ross, 1984); thirdly, adventure games and simulations such as 'Mary Rose' in which children can manipulate events and consider the implications.

However, in the context being assumed here, it will be necessary to examine the possibilities for the design of content-free programs which provide a flexible means of interacting with one's individual structures of knowledge in ways suggested by the use of the 'Focus' program described earlier. Such an interaction may allow children to go beyond the information given and take a step towards emulating the model of the self-organised learner adopted at the Centre for the Study of Human Learning (C.S.H.L.) at Brunel University. Much as one is tempted to flirt with specific curriculum examples, it seems more appropriate to wait until they emerge from the classroom research project introduced above.

Both the above examples, the examination of teachers' constructs in the context of in-service training and the study of children's involvement in book-based aspects of project work, share certain features. The research approaches described are essentially person-centred, making major concessions to the expectations which individuals bring to learning and the meanings which they construct as they learn. There is also a double emphasis on seeking to make explicit the structure of these meanings by the use of the tutor or teacher or researcher who generates a learning conversation to facilitate self-awareness in learning, and to negotiate the possibilities of various kinds of learning referent. Thirdly, the microcomputer has been seen to act as an important vehicle in clarifying the underlying structure of certain kinds of referent in the in-service training context and may well prove to be equally important in this role within the topic context of primary/middle schools.

However, that depends upon the identification of the appropriate type of referent for children. The use of repertory grids with children is full of major uncertainties, as Salmon (1976) warns. Their own writing has an obvious potential as a learning referent, but we need to ask major questions about the ways in which writing can be used and which types are appropriate for reading for learning.

Writing for 'referential' aims

In order to plan effectively for the role of writing in reading for learning to be monitored, the nature of writing being used as a 'referent' needs to be carefully considered, along with the other types which may be used in various complementary ways from time to time. In a recent monograph (Beard, 1984), 'referential' writing has been located within the so-called 'communication triangle' which can be traced back to the work of Aristotle.

Figure 2

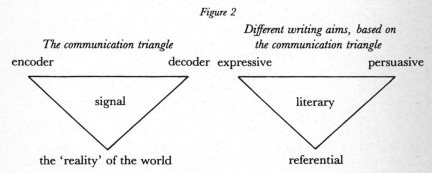

The communication triangle

Different writing aims, based on the communication triangle

This framework of aims comes from a highly scholarly source, Kinneavy (1971,1983) which is not yet well known in the United Kingdom. Kinneavy argues that referential aims of language seek to designate or reproduce the 'reality' of the world. Referential writing can be subdivided into exploratory uses, in which the reality is not known but sought, informative uses and scientific uses in which the information about the world is accompanied by demonstrable proof.

Kinneavy's model provides a very helpful basis for considering the integration of writing into topic work, as it makes explicit the nature and relationships of referential aims and other types. The way in which other aims, such as expressive or literary aims, might complement and enrich the experience of writing for referential aims in topic work is also a matter worthy of serious investigation.

Conclusion

We should not lose sight of the need to continue to ask major questions of the 'what' of topic work. As Eggleston (1984) has recently argued, it is folly to restrict teaching plans for topic work to helping children to acquire facts or skills. From his case study, Eggleston reveals how children acquire concepts and generalisations, even though the teacher had not planned for or monitored these. He argues that once concepts are acquired, different 'isolated' facts are brought together into relationships which give the mind the power to know more and learn more economically.

This kind of approach seems to be particularly appropriate as we look to the new technologies for what they can offer topic work. Vic Kelly's (1984, p. xiv) introduction to a recent book on microcomputers in the curriculum provides a final, challenging link in this chain of argument. Kelly reminds us that 'the major advantage of the microcomputer is not that it can think for one but that it can make one think ... its potential for promoting the development of children's thought processes is enormous.'

References

BEARD, R. F. (1982) *Course evaluation and the repertory grid*. Unpublished Ph.D. thesis, Brunel University Centre for the Study of Human Learning.

BEARD, R. F. (1984) *Children's Writing in the Primary School*, Sevenoaks: Hodder Stoughton Educational.

BROWN, A. L. (1980) 'Metacognitive Development and Reading', in R. J. Spiro *et al.* (eds) *Theoretical Issues in Reading Comprehension*. Hillsdale, N. J.: Erlbaum.

D.E.S. (1975) *A Language for Life* (The Bullock Report). London: H.M.S.O.

D.E.S. (1978) *Primary Education in England*. London: H.M.S.O.

D.E.S. (1982) *Education 5 to 9: An Illustrative Survey of 80 First Schools in England*. London: H.M.S.O.

D.E.S. (1983) *9-13 Middle Schools: An Illustrative Survey*. London: H.M.S.O.

EGGLESTON, J. (1984) 'What did the children learn?'. *Education 3-13*, 12(1), pp.28-32.

GALTON, M., SIMON, B. and CROLL, P. (1980) *Inside the Primary Classroom*. London: Routledge & Kegan Paul.

GOLBY, M. (1982) 'Microcomputers and the primary curriculum', in R. Garland (ed) *Microcomputers and Children in the Primary School*. London: Falmer.

HODGES, M. (1984) 'Topic work: the role of the micro'. *MUSE Report* No. 5.

KELLY, A. V. (ed) (1984) *Microcomputers and the Curriculum*. London: Harper & Row.

KINNEAVY, J. L. (1971) *A theory of Discourse*. Englewood Cliffs, N. J.: Prentice Hall.

KINNEAVY, J. L. (1983) 'A pluralistic synthesis of four contemporary models for teaching composition', in A. Freedman *et al.* (eds) *Learning to Write: First Language/Second Language*. Harlow: Longman.

LUNZER, E. and GARDNER, K. (1984) *Learning from the Written Word*. Edinburgh: Oliver & Boyd.

MARK, J. (1976) *Thunder and Lightnings*. Harmondsworth: Penguin.

MARLAND, M. (1978) 'Responsibility for reading in the secondary school', in L. J. Chapman and P. Czerniewska (eds) *Reading: From Process to Practice*. London: Routledge & Kegan Paul in association with the Open University Press.

MERRITT, J. E. *et al.* (1977) *Developing Independence in Reading* (Open University Course Reading Development (PE231), Block 2). Milton Keynes: The Open University Press.

OTTO, W. and WHITE, S. (eds) (1982) *Reading Expository Material*. New York: Academic Press.

ROSS, A. (1984) 'Learning to hypothesise: a case study of data processing in a primary school classroom', in A. V. Kelly (ed) *Microcomputers and the Curriculum*. London: Harper & Row.

SALMON, P. (1976) 'Grid measures with child subjects', in P. Slater (ed) *The Measurement of Intrapersonal Space by Grid Technique: Volume 1, Explorations of Intrapersonal Space*. London: Wiley.

STENHOUSE, L. (1975) *An Introduction to Curriculum Research and Development*. London: Heinemann.

SUPRAMANIAM, S. and BEARD, R. F. (1982) *From Fluent Reading to Comprehension*. Milton Keynes: The Open University Press.

8   Testing reading: recent developments

Peter D. Pumfrey

Thirty years ago, Guilford, an eminent psychologist, educator and research worker commented that 'No other contribution of psychology has had the soical impact equal to that created by the psychological test. No other technique and no other body of theory has been so fully rationalised from the mathematical point of view.' At that time he was speaking of the then conventional normative test theory. Subsequent developments in the field of criterion-referenced mastery testing have shown that conventional test theory was but one of several complementary positions in this field.

Theoretical controversies also abound concerning the nature of reading abilities, their development and the implications for the learning and teaching of reading. For example, those professionals favouring a 'top down' model of reading development, whereby the sub-skills of reading are acquired by the act of reading, are faced by others who argue for the validity of a sub-skills approach to the acquisition of more complex skills. Fortunately the two positions are not mutually exclusive although the polarisation that sometimes appears in the popular press suggests otherwise. Articulated and explicit positions concerning the measurement of reading abilities and their nature are essential to the resolution of such pedagogic concerns.

Thoughts on the Cause of the Present Discontents is not the title of a book by Arthur Scargill or Ian McGregor. Neither was it a 'leaked' Cabinet Paper nor even a chapter in Sir Keith Joseph's memoirs. It does contain a salutary warning to those educationists who find the measurement of reading abilities and processes an all absorbing professional activity. I quote:' ''Not men but measures'': a sort of charm by which many people get loose from every honourable engagement'. These words of Edmund Burke written in the eighteenth century and in a different context are a reminder that those interested in the measurement of reading abilities and processes should note. Beware the spurious precision and questionable simplicities whereby figures and statistics are presented as clarifications but in effect act as smokescreens. Beware equally the attitude that rejects the measurement of reading abilities as an unimportant activity.

Our function as professional specialists in reading is to provide effective services at various levels. The ability to read is both a contributor to and a determinant of cognitive and emotional development. To be unable to read in our society is to be progressively disadvantaged. Long ago William Godwin expressed the positive side of this issue when he wrote 'He that loves reading has everything within his reach. He has but to desire and he may possess himself of every species of wisdom to judge and power to perform.' The power to read is an amplifier of human abilities. Computer literacy is but another facet of the latter. A heavy boulder may be immovable until we use a lever. A problem may be insurmountable until we gain access, via reading, to the accumulated knowledge and wisdom of our culture.

Our aims include helping optimise reading attainments, not maximising them. To do this we each have a professional duty to be *more* than an effective individual. We must be able to communicate our ideas, our practices, our successes and our failures. This demands that we be explicit and precise rather than intuitive and vague. The continuing challenge faced by all of us is to describe our theoretical ideas concerning the nature of reading abilities and their acquisition, to predict developments and to minimise avoidable reading difficulties.

Without a variety of reading tests and assessment techniques, the task could not be done. It cannot be said too frequently that reading (or other) tests and assessment techniques are no more than efficient, reliable, valid and public means of obtaining information. The value of such information is that it helps us to make better decisions than would otherwise be the case. It helps us to describe what we are doing, why we are doing it and to test the validity of our description. It enables us to predict changes and to check our predictions. It guides us in modifying circumstances so as to increase the likelihood of improving reading attainments.

In these endeavours the collection, generation and analysis, availability and utility of information obtained from reading tests and assessment techniques has frequently been restricted. Information technology can dramatically reduce such limitations (Mason, Blanchard and Daniel, 1983).

This paper examines some of the effects of information technology in general and of microcomputer applications in particular; they are considered in relation to the testing of reading. Both currently available systems and others still in the pilot stage will be described.

The use of reading tests and assessment techniques has increased markedly in Britain over the last decade (Gipps *et al*, 1983). The variety of approaches to assessment has also risen. We live in an age when 'accountability' is increasingly demanded of the teaching profession (Lord, 1984). Reading tests and assessment techniques are means whereby this professional responsibility can be demonstrated to the various groups and individuals who have legitimate interests in children's reading attainments and attitudes towards reading. Will developments in information technology help or hinder in this endeavour?

Microcomputers and the testing of reading

The central concept of the contemporary electronic computer was contained in the design and development work of Charles Babbage, the Cambridge mathematician (1790–1871). His machine was designed to solve the Astronomer Royal's need for a means of rapidly and accurately computing nautical tables. It was the limitations of the technology of that era that prevented the full implementation of Babbage's concept. Not until 1945 was the first electronic computer developed at the University of Pennsylvania.

That computer contained about 18,000 valves. The heat that they generated and their breakdown rate severely restricted the utility of the device to all potential users. The invention of the transistor in 1947 largely solved the heat and reliability problems. However, it was not until the development of the integrated circuit, whereby complex circuitry is printed, or etched, onto very small discs or squares of silica, popularly known as 'chips', that the development of computers as we now know them began in earnest.

Means of converting data and questions into commands that the computer could follow to process the former and answer the latter led to the development of programs known as data processing languages or 'author languages'. As early as 1969 there were at least 60 of these. By 1980, one language had become dominant in the microcomputer field. It is called Beginner All-purpose Symbolic Instruction Code and popularly known by the acronym Basic. Most of the software available for use in schools is written for micro-computers that use Basic. Whilst it is likely to continue to be the most commonly used language at this level, more powerful ones will increasingly intrude. So will languages devised for particular purposes. Logo, developed by Seymour Papert, will probably become the language for children. Their teachers are likely to be required to learn it. Pilot, a language used in writing lessons, is seen by some authorities as one which all teachers 'may well be expected to master' (Mason, Blanchard and Daniel, 1983).

This section of the paper is largely based on information from the following sources.

(1)   A specially requested computer search of the literature on the use of microcomputers in the testing of reading. The search was carried out by the E.R.I.C. Clearinghouse on Tests, Measurement and Evaluation based at the Educational Testing Service at Princeton, New Jersey.

(2)   The second edition of a book published by the International Reading Association entitled *Computer Applications in Reading* (Mason, Blanchard and Daniel, 1983). This book is a mine of information on all aspects of computers and reading. It contains 910 annotated references.

(3)   The many test publishers from around the world who have sent me details of the uses they make of computers in constructing reading tests. Additionally, publishers have provided much information on systems in which the testing and teaching of reading are integrated.

(4)   The American Guidance Service who kindly sent me some software. This demonstrates a relatively unsophisticated but time-saving program that can be used in conjunction with the *Woodcock Reading Mastery Tests* (Schultz, 1982).

(5)   Colleagues at the National Foundation for Educational Research, the Godfrey Thomson Unit at the University of Edinburgh and those at the Assessment of Performance Unit of the Department of Education and Science.

(6)   Staff of the Microelectronics Education Project at Newcastle-upon-

Tyne and at the Special Education Microelectronics Resource Centre in Manchester.

One way of finding out what a microcomputer can do in testing reading is to make up a simple test containing a few items. Then find out how you can get the microcomputer to display the items on the visual display unit (V.D.U.). A multiple-choice sentence completion test would make a good starting point. Getting the system to record the reader's responses, to summarise, analyse and present them is, in my experience, initially extremely frustrating but eventually valuable. If possible, obtain the help of a teenager studying programming.

The microcomputer in your school can help you construct reading tests. There are available programs that will guide you in preparing, for example, multiple-choice, cloze and matching item type tests. The microcomputer can also record responses, score, analyse and summarise test results and point to interpretation – provided that the software is compatible with your machine. The system will enable local norms on tests to be accumulated and changes in the reading attainments of individuals and groups to be monitored.

A major danger is that data can be collected and generated without a clear understanding of the purposes to which it is to be put. School systems and government departments are awash with statistical data. If we fail to reflect on the reading test data that are currently being collected on a massive scale, we do our pupils and ourselves a disservice. Collecting reading test results can become a self-perpetuating activity providing few benefits to clients. Fortunately, this need not be the case.

Uses

From a vast and varied array of development, four have been selected for mention here. Each represents a different aspect of the use of microcomputers in the testing of reading. Each has implications for the classroom teacher. Do not, however, assume that the software will be compatible with your particular microcomputer. On the positive side, it is likely that it will be in time, provided that the program proves of value.

(i) The matching of reader and text requires an assessment of the child's reading attainment and of the difficulty of the text. With respect to the latter point, some years ago the U.K.R.A. used a computerised system to assess the readability of children's books, moderating the results with teachers' appraisals. There is a plethora of formulae for assessing text readability. A recent British book called *Readability in the Classroom* gives details of nine measures. The book also contains a computer program for estimating readability (Harrison, 1980). The development of a computer program using five different readability formulae has also been described recently (Feldman *et al.*, 1983). A central problem to be solved, if there is to be a satisfactory pupil/test match, is that of assessing the child's reading ability on the same scale as that of the readability formulae used to assess the text. Rasch scaling is one approach that attempts to deal with this issue. In the U.S.A., the College

Board's system *Degrees of Reading Power* places students' reading comprehension scores on the same scale as textual difficulty. It is claimed that the readability formula used is based on the 'most technically valid one available'. This is deemed to be the mean cloze formula developed by Bormuth (1969). A software program for schools has been developed that will enable schools rapidly to establish indices of Degrees of Reading Power for any locally produced material. The College Board's *1983-1984 Readability Report* provides 262 pages of information on the readability levels of a wide range of materials.

On reflection, we have a classic example of a mismatch between what *could be* done and what *is* done in the teaching of reading. With the current book allowance per pupil per annum in Britain as low as it is, even when we know what books children require, the resources to ensure that the books are provided are not available. On the positive side, a system such as *Degrees of Reading Power* might generate the public and political awareness that will make the necessary funds available.

(ii) Mason *et al.* (1983) refer to an article entitled 'Talk and type'. A program has been developed that allows users to type only the *first* letter of each word *as they speak*. The machine types the rest. It is reported that an experienced typer–speaker can exceed 160 words per minute with 99 per cent accuracy. The system requires that initially users must orally enter every word in the system's vocabulary. Presumably this is needed in order that the recognition system can function. At present it is unlikely that such a program could work using the limited capacity of a typical school microcomputer.

As early as 1977 a device with the trade name 'Optacon' enabled blind persons to read ordinary print. The user moved a small camera across the text with one hand. Under the fingers of the other hand the shapes of the letters were reproduced through a series of vibrating rods. In 1984, this seems almost antediluvian, such is the rate of technological development. In a related field, Mason *et al.* (1983) refer to the work of W. H. Earle with a child only able to control her eyes. Using a computer-controlled device, she now has a 'voice' and 'writing capability'.

One development that will have a significant impact on the interactive testing and teaching of reading will be the arrival of machines which, when linked to a computerised speech synthesiser, will read aloud printed text.

(iii) Means of helping teachers acquire diagnostic testing skills in reading are being explored. Computer-based simulated cases have been used as a means of teaching reading diagnosis. In one study, five simulated case studies are presented and a program of computer-assisted instruction ensures that students collect data systematically using diagnostic reports and checklists. The students' diagnoses are then compared with expert opinion. The advantages claimed are that students can practise on a large number of representative case studies because equivalent forms of the five case studies are available.

Is this a good idea or a suspect one? In view of the variety of interpretations made by reading experts from the same case study material, one has reservations concerning the validity of such a venture (Visonhaler *et al.*, 1983). On the positive side, the explicit nature of computerised training in diagnostic skills helps to remove the fog of idiosyncratic professional subjectivity that often hinders communication between reading diagnosticians. When the efficacy of such training is validated against the alleviation of real children's reading difficulties, one will feel more confident concerning this particular application.

(iv) The *Woodcock Reading Mastery Tests* combine criterion-referenced and normative information with performance levels related to Informal Reading Inventory (I.R.I.) criteria. Criterion-referenced tests are of two major types. One of these is a content-referenced scale and assesses the child's performance on that scale. The other type of criterion-referenced reading test is based on an 'expectancy statement'. Such a test predicts, on a probabilistic basis, the child's likelihood of success in situations involving reading materials of differing difficulty levels. In the *Woodcock Reading Mastery Tests*, both types of criterion-referenced test are available. Additionally, the author has devised a special scale which is considered to be a joint norm-referenced and criterion-referenced scale. This scale predicts the pupil's *relative* percentage mastery on reading tasks at various grade levels and links with I.R.I. criteria. The instrument is an individual diagnostic test that assesses five skills: letter recognition; word recognition; word attack; word comprehension and passage comprehension. A combination of all five sub-scales provides a measure of what is called total reading power. The test comes in two forms and covers the age range from 5 to 18 years. The test uses Rasch scaling and therefore has the advantage that both item difficulties and the test scores of pupils may be placed on a common scale of equal units. The mastery scales indicate the likelihood of success of a pupil on a reading task of a given difficulty. In addition, the test provides a direct link with the I.R.I. criteria as defined by Betts (1946), and normative data can be obtained (Woodcock, 1973).

In 1982 a microcomputer program that can be used with this test was developed. It requires an Apple II Plus computer with 48K memory and using Disk Operating System (D.O.S.) 3.3. The full title of the program is 'Automated System for Scoring and Interpreting Standardised Tests'. Its acronym is 'ASSIST'. The program does not administer the test: its function is to take the drudgery out of the recording, cumulation and analysis of the test data.

In computer language, 'menu' refers to the operations that the program will carry out. The 'ASSIST' program offers three choices:

(1) 'Student Report' program;
(2) 'Class Report' program; and
(3) 'Student Graphic Profile' program.

The system is linked to a printer so that once all the information required has been displayed on the V.D.U. it can be saved and /or printed, if required.

Having typed in the individual pupils' scores, the 'Student Report' program displays the information in Figure 1 on the V.D.U. and, if so instructed, will print it.

The 'Class Report' prints the analyses for a group of pupils whose scores are

Figure 1

ASSIST STUDENT REPORT

NAME: TEST: (pre v. post)

TEST DATE: GRADE:

FORM: REPORT DATE:

TEST	EASY READING LEVEL	READING GRADE SCORE	FAILURE READING LEVEL	RELATIVE MASTERY SCORE	PERCENTILE RANK	NORMAL CURVE EQUIVALENT
LETTER IDENTN.						
WORD IDENTN.						
WORD ATTACK.						
WORD COMPR.						
PASSAGE COMPR.						
TOTAL READING.						

on file. The pupils' names are printed on the left-hand side of the printed output, and the six test scores are arranged horizontally. Information concerning only one aspect of the scoring system can be displayed at a time. The system will allow the progress of pupils, and the differences between their scores on two occasions on each of the variables, to be displayed. Additionally, a graphical display of a pupil's pre-test and post-test percentile ranks on the tests can be presented on the V.D.U. The information cannot, however, be printed.

The 'ASSIST' program has been described because it brings together a number of important issues. Firstly, the test includes many novel aspects of measurement theory and test construction in the field of reading. It is criterion-referenced, normative and related to the I.R.I. criteria. Secondly, the computer program demonstrates a number of ways in which a considerable amount of time can be saved in analysing the results of the test.

Limitations

To become familiar with what is available in relation to the testing of reading using microcomputers will require both time and opportunity. We must become literate – computer literate. This involves ability, knowledge and understanding:

1.   the ability to use and instruct computers to aid in learning, solving problems and managing information;

2.   knowledge of functions, applications, capabilities, limitations and social implications of computers and related technology; and
3.   understanding needed to learn and evaluate new applications and social issues as they arise. (Educational Testing Service, 1984)

In education we are always short of time. We also do not have sufficient funds to purchase the range and variety of testing and teaching materials that would enable us to optimise pupils' reading attainments. If reading teachers are to become computer literate, large-scale in-service programmes will have to be provided locally.

Technological limitations include the glare problems associated with prolonged reading from a V.D.U. The relative scarcity of microcomputers in school and their lack of portability are further problems. They can be overcome. To do so would be expensive. As a country, have we the will to make the necessary funds available? Looking to the immediate future of an information technology dominated society, dare we do otherwise?

Promise

There is little doubt that information technology, including computer-assisted learning and computer-assisted instruction, will increasingly pervade our lives. A degree of control of the construction of reading tests exists that was hitherto unknown. The collection, storage, analysis and interpretation of reading test data has moved to a new plane. Developments are moving rapidly. The hardware exists; it is not there that the limitations mainly lie. We must help with the software (Weiss, 1983).

Seymour Papert once wrote 'It is better for the child to be a programmer than to be programmed.' There is a message for all of us.

Conclusion

In the introduction to this paper, the question was asked 'Will developments in information technology help or hinder our endeavours to become more professionally competent and accountable?' In relation to the testing of reading, the technology represents a challenge to the profession. Any challenge contains both opportunities and problems. If we are to capitalise on the former to the advantage of our clients, we must master the microcomputer. To many members of the teaching profession such a prospect is daunting. Partly this is because of the technical language used, its unfamiliarity and the 'in-group' shorthand and jargon that put off potential users. For example, is it necessary to know the difference between a bit, a byte and a nibble? Before decimalisation, we learned during our education that '12 inches equal one foot and three feet equal one yard'. Do we now have to learn that 4 bits equal one nibble and 2 nibbles equal one byte? Fortunately, the answer is a resounding 'No'.

Today the internal combustion engine and its use in cars is taken for granted. It has had profound consequences on our experience of the country in which we live and of the world. However, our understanding of cars can be at a number of levels. Most of us use cars as a means to an end. A smaller number understand the workings of the engine. An even smaller number of individuals explore the basic sciences involved.

Microcomputers in schools are a tool we are having to learn about at one or more of the same three levels. The reading teacher's undoubted expertise must be incorporated into the computer software that is being developed in relation to reading tests and assessment techniques. The translation of current written and oral instruments into disk format is only the initial step in what promises to be an exciting journey.

Two of the most powerful forces against the reading teacher capitalising on the promise of the microcomputer in the testing of reading are the inertia of habit and the fear of change. Professor Wragg of the University of Exeter has recently commented (lightheartedly) on such phenomena. Wragg proposes founding the Society of Logjammers, Obstructionists, Thwarters and Hinderers, to be known by the acronym 'SLOTH'. It is assumed that members of a pre-existing underground group identified as 'Staffroom Early Palaeolithic Obstructionists' will be founder members. In spelling out the strategies this group has used to prevent or delay innovation in education, Wragg has performed an important service. Some reading teachers and research workers manifest a Luddite-like mentality in relation to microcomputers in schools. It is contended that these are in a minority. The vast majority will accept the challenge of contributing to the development of the interactive testing of reading. With our involvement, we can hasten the day when the microcomputer will take over most of the white-collar ditch digging associated with the testing of reading.

References

BETTS, E. A. (1946) *Foundations of Reading Instruction*. New York: American Book.

BORMUTH, J. R. (1969) *Development of Readability Analyses*. Final report. Project Number OEG-3-7-070052-0326. Washington, D. C.: Office of Education, Bureau of Research, U.S. Department of Health, Education and Welfare.

EDUCATIONAL TESTING SERVICE (1984) 'What is computer literacy?' *ETS Developments*, Spring, p.9.

FELDMAN, P. *et al.* (1983) 'Using microcomputers to determine readability levels'. *Reading Improvement*, 20(2), pp.82–6.

GIPPS, C., STEADMAN, S., BLACKSTONE, T. and STIERER, B. (1983) *Testing Children: Standardised Testing in Local Education Authorities and Schools*. London: Heinemann Educational.

HARRISON, C. (1980) *Readability in the Classroom*. Cambridge: C.U.P.

LORD, R. (1984) *Value for Money in Education*. London: Chartered Institute of Public Finance and Accountancy.

MASON, G. E., BLANCHARD, J. S. and DANIEL, D. B. (1983) *Computer Applications in Reading (2nd Edn.)*. Neward: International Reading Association.

SCHULTZ, S. J. (1982) *ASSIST for the Woodcock Reading Mastery Tests, Forms A and B.* (For use with Apple II Plus computers with 48K memory and DOS 3.3.). Circle Pines, Minn.: American Guidance Service.

VISONHALER, J. S., WEINSHANK, A. B., WAGNER, C. C. and POLIN, R. W.

(1983) 'Diagnosing children with educational problems: characteristics of reading and learning disabilities specialists and classroom teachers'. *Reading Research Quarterly*, XVIII (2), pp.134–64.

WEISS, D. J. (ed) (1983) *New Horizons in Testing: Latent Trait Test Theory and Computerised Adaptive Testing*. London: Academic Press.

WOODCOCK, R. W. (1973) *Woodcock Reading Mastery Tests*. Circle Pines, Minn.: American Guidance Service.

9   Approaches to reading remediation: an assessment of new and old techniques

Gilbert R. Gredler

New technologies for the teaching of reading are being emphasised today in education. The use of computer technology is increasingly touted as a means of improving the child's reading performance. A number of concerns have been raised as to the value of computers in education. It is frequently suggested that they are nothing more than 'expensive page turners' and in effect mimic programmed instruction books (Oettinger, 1969). The question can also be raised as to whether it is a worthwhile goal just to have elementary school children performing two to three grade/age levels above their current level. Does such performance 'pay off' in secondary school? Is the measure of 'true' education one where more knowledge is just learned in a shorter period of time? Also, is it of value to ascertain whether effective instruction can be provided within a shorter time limit? Individuals within Western society spend an average of 12–14 years of their lives within educational institutions. It would certainly seem important to utilise educational instructional approaches which could possibly provide effective instruction within a shorter time period and thereby be more cost efficient. These same questions need to be asked in regard to children with learning problems. Can use of computer-assisted instruction (C.A.I.) become a productive part of remediation efforts?

Use of C.A.I. in beginning reading

One of the first C.A.I. studies undertaken has provided detailed analysis of its value with 6-year-old children (Fletcher and Atkinson, 1972). The reading performance of 50 matched pairs of children at the end of first grade was examined, with one child of each pair receiving C.A.I. in reading, the other child receiving the regular classroom instruction. Computer-assisted instruction was provided for a five-month time period during the first grade but the children received no such instruction while in their second year of school. The instructional sequence was limited to 12 minutes per day. Except for this 12-minute period of C.A.I. the school day was similar to that of the control group. Standardised test results administered at the end of the first year indicated an average increase of 5·05 months over that of the control group. Test results at the end of the second grade reflected a difference of 4·90 months in favour of the C.A.I. group who had had no intervening C.A.I. treatment.

Even more important was the fact that, while the reading performance of both boys and girls improved when exposed to C.A.I., the relative rate of improvement was greater for the boys. This is an important result since in most American schools boys lag behind girls at the end of the first and second grades.

It should also be noted that the boys who received the supplementary C.A.I. instruction out-performed the girls who received traditional first grade instruction. This is one small piece of evidence that demonstrates that beginning differences in reading achievement which favour girls can be altered.

This study also indicates that supplementary instruction was needed to reinforce the instructional programme offered in the regular classroom. Atkinson (1974) states that C.A.I. should not necessarily be utilised in all phases of reading instruction. He considers that C.A.I. provides individualised instruction which cannot be matched by the teacher even when working with a group composed of only four or five children. Atkinson attributes the better performance of the girls to the predominance of female teachers in the school and also because girls are better at memorising, which in turn helps them to cope with a curriculum which emphasises sight word procedures. The result of this C.A.I. study is similar to what has been found by a host of other investigations: that normal instruction when supplemented by C.A.I. is more effective than normal classroom instruction alone (Edwards *et al.*, 1975).

But some reading specialists have raised questions about Atkinson's approach to beginning reading instruction. Spache (1967) states that the computer-assisted programme offered by Atkinson denigrates the reading process by overemphasis on letter identification and discrimination; presentation of words with matching pictures without providing a meaningful context; and in general concentrating on the decoding aspects of reading to the 'exclusion of the important process of encoding or reacting'. However, a more recent approach to beginning reading instruction which would appear to answer many of Spache's concerns is that of the Writing to Read project. Designed to aid young children to learn to read more effectively, it is currently being field tested on 10,000 children in the U.S.A. In this programme, children learn to write words by combining the 42 phonemes into words. Students learn to spell the words phonemically. The computer provides a high degree of individual attention as well as multisensory experience in constructing words. Words are typed into the computer; the children see the word constructed on the monitor and then they repeat the phonemes along with the computer voice (Rotenberg, 1984).

The programme is composed of three parts: a computer program in which the child is led through a sequenced, self-paced cycle of interacting learning; work journals which reinforce their activities and are similar to the computer program and a language development programme which provides the child with a number of different activities to apply the language arts skills.

Preliminary results of this approach to beginning reading are found in standardised test results from the Wake County, North Carolina, school system. Mean scores at the end of first grade reading of the C.A.I. children were at the 89th percentile in comparison to the control group's score at the 69th percentile.

Substitution of C.A.I. for traditional instruction

Mixed results have been noted when C.A.I. was substituted for conventional instruction. As many studies indicated no difference between the two forms of instruction as showed gains. However a number of studies indicated that while the use of C.A.I. did not result in higher achievement levels on the part of students, the time it took them to learn was significantly reduced (Edwards *et al.*, 1975). Edward's review of the results of C.A.I. included school populations that ranged from first grade through college-age students. It is therefore difficult to generalise about C.A.I. effectiveness from studies of such diverse age groups and which involve quite different curricula and software materials.

C.A.I. with learning disabled children

There have been very few studies of the use of C.A.I. with children retarded in reading or maths and designated as 'learning disabled'. One of the most detailed studies was carried out recently in Phoenix, Arizona, schools using the entire population of 205 'learning disabled' children who had been identified from the school population in grades 1 to 6 (McDermott and Watkins, 1983).

Computer-assisted instruction was provided through a microcomputer program which covered fundamental to advanced elementary maths and word spelling skills. Instruction continued during one whole school year from September through May. In the experimental group C.A.I. was substituted for the same amount of time devoted to spelling/maths instruction in the conventional group. Results indicated 'no clear advantage over traditional remedial instruction for elementary and junior high level children who are learning impaired'. McDermott and Watkins suggest that various combinations of computerised and conventional remedial instruction will be needed and that the success rate will also vary partially as a function of the severity of the learning problems encountered and the different learning styles encountered.

The rationale for use of C.A.I.

A number of different reasons have been enunciated as to why C.A.I. might be effective. These include:

(a) With use of C.A.I. there is a better adaptation to the pace of the student (Martin, 1973).
(b) Immediate information is provided the student as to the correctness of his or her response. In other words, immediate knowledge of results or feedback is important (Annelli, 1977).
(c) Machine instructions can more easily clarify the problem and provide the 'required freqency and subtlety of reinforcement' which is needed (Skinner, 1972).
(d) C.A.I. makes more effective provision for active and passive feedback

during learning sequences than does conventional instruction (Annelli, 1977). Immediate feedback to the student aids in the correction of errors.

(e)   Annelli (1977) states that one reason lower S.E.S. children are poor readers may be because they do not attend to the relevant learning task for an extended period of time. She feels it is possible that effective C.A.I. helps to increase the attention span of the child more than what is found in conventional instruction and thus the child is actively responding to learning tasks for a longer time.

(f)   Effective C.A.I. provides a better opportunity to implement 'distributed practice' sessions. Such sessions help to reduce the amount of forgetting by the child (Ausubel, 1968; Annelli, 1977). One of the variables which needs to be further investigated is the amount of time which should be given over to C.A.I. in the regular classroom. Annelli found that C.A.I. sessions ranged in length from 5 to 45 minutes. C.A.I. beyond a set time often leads to boredom.

(g)   The type of material presented will have a bearing on the length of the C.A.I. sessions. Annelli states that drill and practice sessions which are obviously quite repetitive in nature are probably more effective in short sessions. More lengthy sessions may overwhelm or bore the student.

(h)   The effectiveness of C.A.I. obviously will be partially determined by the type of 'software' utilised. There is considerable variation in the quality of curricula and material available and to date there has been insufficient analysis of this material.

(i)   Organisational factors also have a bearing on the use and acceptance of C.A.I.

For example, one study of the effectiveness of C.A.I. with third and fourth grade children of low S.E.S. background in Newark, N. J., indicated that the children in the C.A.I. groups performed no more effectively in reading than those in conventional instruction groups (Annelli, 1977). It was pointed out that some of the vocabulary and reading comprehension material used in the C.A.I. phase was at a lower difficulty level than items included on the standardised reading tests. Few of the teachers involved in the study attended the C.A.I. workshop offered to acquaint school personnel about the nature of C.A.I. and those that did attend said the sessions were not helpful.

If such negative attitudes spilled over in the teachers' work with their students, it is possible that there was less discussion of C.A.I. lessons in class and less use of diagnostic printouts by the teachers. Annelli states, 'teachers were distressed about the disrupting effect C.A.I. had on classroom scheduling'.

Some questions to ask

Evidence from the use of two programs in beginning reading, that of Fletcher and Atkinson (1972) and that of Martin (1973), indicate that C.A.I.

does indeed 'pay off' in improvement of performance in reading of young children. However, it would be erroneous to state that C.A.I. should be the preferred approach to the teaching of reading. Any reading programme, if properly structured and organised, should be able to produce important gains in the children's learning performance. For example, it has been demonstrated that the use of the 'Sound Start' program of Murphy and Sullivan with kindergarten children resulted in important gains in pre-reading skills (Oliver, 1980). Teachers were able to provide each child with direct instruction, this instruction taking place over 100 days of the 180-day school year and averaging 71 minutes per day. This programme was carried out in eight lower S.E.S. schools in Cambridge, Massachusetts. By the end of kindergarten, two-thirds of the children reached or exceeded the phonics inventory norms for the top one-third of beginning first grade children.

In another study Erskine (1972) identified key children who would be at risk for reading. These children then received a diagnostic prescriptive programme of reading readiness activities for two 45-minute sessions per week for a total of 16 weeks. Erskine concentrated on activities which would be considered to strengthen underlying ability clusters of these kindergarten students. Improved readiness test scores of these target children led Erskine to state that this was a worthwhile approach in preparing children for reading activities.

Summary

Computer-assisted instruction as exemplified by the program devised by Fletcher and Atkinson (1972), and Martin (1973) succeed by:

(a) providing a multisensory approach to learning letters and words;
(b) allowing the child to become active in the learning process through composing his or her own sentences and stories;
(c) providing a patient, supportive environment without negative feedback;
(d) monitoring in a more effective and efficient manner the practice and drill sessions which all students need.

Traditional instruction does provide drill and practice sessions but frequently such sessions are poorly organised and composed of boring 'make work' exercises while C.A.I. presents the practice material within a more novel framework and in a context where immediate corrective feedback is provided. Therefore, the child's motivational level is higher. C.A.I. provides an effective follow-up correction stage by closely monitoring the child's performance.

Since many children with reading problems have experienced anxiety, discouragement and fear of failure, the affective element in the learning situation must always be at the forefront in planning the educational programme of these children. Examples of remediation programs which involve sophisticated curricula programming can be seen in the work of Burkholder (1968)

84

who used an I.T.P.A. curriculum to provide effective remediation to second and third grade children in the Tucson, Arizona, schools; the counselling program of Lawrence (1974) in his program with 9- and 10-year olds in Taunton, England, and the Temple University remediation program with second grade children in the parochial schools of Philadelphia (Gredler, 1978). This program involved the use of Stott's Programmed Reading Kit which is well known as providing a structured approach to many of the tasks of reading within a novel game framework.

Another aspect of reading remediation which is seldom discussed is the question of how much instruction children receive in the classroom during the day and also how much remedial instruction is given to students when they are placed in such a programme. In one study 35 second grade children from ten different schools in a Minnesota school system were observed during their scheduled reading periods. Observations were made in the classrooms of 26 teachers. Worksheets took most of the time set aside for teaching of reading, averaging 27 minutes a day. Active teaching took up an average of 18 minutes a day. There was wide variability in teaching individual students, with one student receiving less than two minutes of instruction in a day (1·8) while another child received 39 minutes (Thurlow, *et al.*, 1984). In summary, it was found that of 120 minutes of time scheduled for reading activities, 80 minutes was actually allocated to reading. The average student was involved only 20 minutes per day in making active academic responses, with only eight minutes of that time devoted to silent reading and two minutes to oral reading. The other 40 minutes of the reading period was spent on what was called 'task management' and 'waiting' responses. Thurlow points out that, if instruction continued at this daily rate, only 21 hours of one school year would be devoted to reading silently and five hours to reading aloud.

Thus, it needs to be asked whether the regular classroom is indeed providing sufficient instructional time effectively to help the children to learn the curricula material. In the I.T.P.A. remediation project Burkholder (1968) provided 20 hours of active instruction; in the Philadelphia remediation program students were provided 15 hours of instruction (Gredler, 1978), and Oliver (1980), when using a phonics program with kindergarten children, provided 118 hours of instructional time.

One important variable which all the special programmes described here provide is much more instructional time than is given in the regular class. In the future when other studies are undertaken as to the effectiveness of a particular teaching method, a separate analysis will need to be undertaken of the time spent on instruction in the regular classroom.

References

ANNELLI, C. M. (1977) 'Computer assistant instruction and reading achievement of urban third and fourth graders'. Unpublished doctoral dissertation, Rutgers University.
AUSUBEL, D. P. (1968) *Educational Psychology: A Cognitive View*. New York: Holt, Reinhart & Winston.

ATKINSON, R. C. (1974) 'Teaching children to read using a computer'. *American Psychologist*, 29, pp.169–78.

BURKHOLDER, R. B. (1968) 'The improvement of reading ability through the development of specific underlying or associated mental abilities'. Unpublished doctoral dissertation, University of Arizona.

EDWARDS, J., NORTON, S., TAYLOR, S., WEISS, M. and DUSSELDORP, R. (1975) *Educational Leadership*, 33, pp.147–53.

ERSKINE, R. G. (1972) 'Developing reading potential: identification and instruction of disadvantaged high risk readers in kindergarten'. Unpublished doctoral dissertation, Purdue University.

FLETCHER, J. D. and ATKINSON, R. C. (1972) 'Evaluation of the Stanford CAI program in initial reading'. *Journal of Educational Psychology*, 63, pp.597–602.

GREDLER, G. R. (1978) 'Learning disabilities and reading disorders: a current assessment'. *Psychology in the Schools*, 15, pp.226–38.

LAWRENCE, D. (1974) 'The effects of counselling on retarded readers'. *Educational Research*, 13, pp.119–24.

MARTIN, J. (1973) *Design of Man–Computer Dialogues*. Englewood Cliffs, N. J.: Prentice-Hall.

McDERMOTT. P. A. and WATKINS, M. W. (1983) 'Computerized vs. conventional remedial instruction for learning disabled pupils'. *Journal of Special Education*, 17, pp.81–8.

OETTINGER, A. G. (1969) *Run, Computer Run: The Mythology of Educational Innovation*. New York: Collier.

OLIVER, L. S. (1980) 'The effects of extended instructional time on the readiness for reading of kindergarten children'. Unpublished doctoral dissertation, Boston University.

ROTENBERG, L. (1984) 'Booting up for reading'. *Teaching & Computers*, 1, pp.16–19.

SKINNER, B. F. (1972) *Cumulative Record: A Selection of Papers*. New York: Appleton Century Crofts Meredith.

SPACHE, G. D. (1967) 'A reaction to computer-assisted instruction in initial reading: the Stanford project'. *Reading Research Quarterly*, 3, pp.101–9.

THURLOW, M., GRADEN, J., YSSELDYKE, J. and ALOGZZINE, R. (1984) 'Student reading during reading class: the lost activity in reading instruction'. *Journal of Educational Research*, 77, pp.267–72.

10   Cohesion and the micro

John Chapman

In a paper given to the Fifth Conference of the Australian Reading Association in August 1979, I reviewed developments in our understanding of reading and its teaching at the turn of the decade. At that time, as well as looking back I also looked forward and in doing so I predicted that the study of reading in the eighties would be dominated by two powerful forces. One would be academic, and would emanate from the burgeoning field of text-linguistics and the other technological, the advent of the microcomputer.

It is interesting now, some five years later, to review those 'Prospects for the eighties' as I called them (Chapman, 1980) and to judge their impact on reading. In order to do this I will first suggest what their present status is and then show how together they could become a very powerful force for both the academic study of reading and its teaching.

The advance of microcomputer technology

There is hardly any need to draw attention to the popularity of today's inexpensive microcomputers. In particular the growth of the home or personal computer market has been of considerable proportions.

Indeed, it is claimed that in the U.K. there are more home or personal microcomputers per head of the population than anywhere else in the world. When I looked at the possible growth in the numbers of microcomputers in 1979, I had in mind something quite different. I envisaged then a growing number of teacher enthusiasts using microcomputers in their classrooms. Today practically every school has one and the popular press carries information and advice about home and personal computers. The educational potential of this development is enormous and has already begun to alter the nature of the experiences of the children in our schools. Children in infant departments are already familiar with these machines and some are able to operate them. Some already have a great deal of the technical vocabulary that surrounds the computer world: they appreciate, for example, that to press 'return' is a command that causes the computer to respond, in most cases they meet with.

In the same way, therefore, as we take other environmental factors into consideration, we now have to accept additional problems with this new generation of children, for there will be an additional kind of deprivation. There will be many children coming to school in the eighties who didn't get a 'Sinclair in their stocking'!

Be that as it may, will this really matter? After all it may be a fact that will pass away like many another. I would like to suggest that it really will matter and for two serious fundamental reasons. Althought both these points have been made elsewhere by Anderson (1984b), they need reinforcing.

The first point is to do with the control of information. This can be illustrated by an event from the past. In an interesting paper, Anderson quoting McShane (1983) recalls how the Aztec empire fell with apparent ease to a handful of Spaniards. A very important contributory cause in their victory was the destruction of the Aztec's information store house. An empire, then in all its glory, had been built up by establishing a central control of the flow of information. The empire was wiped out it seems, not only by the Spaniards' musket power, the usual reason given, but by the crippling effect of being deprived of information.

Associated with the control of information is the speed at which information is transmitted. This can also be illustrated from history, this time from our own. An account relates how through receiving early knowledge of the result of the battle of Waterloo long before anyone else, the Rothschilds were able to increase their wealth considerably. The story has it that the news of the defeat of Napoleon was brought by the carrier pigeons and a fortune was amassed by a few swift moves on the stock exchange (Naisbitt, 1984). Communication satellites and computers now bring information from and to all parts of the world virtually instantaneously and such advantages exploited by the Rothschilds have ceased. However, the key now lies with those who control computer networks.

The age in which we now live has been called an 'information' age (Naisbitt, 1984) and those who control the flow of information will be in the ascendancy. Central to this is the computer. It is important therefore that we have a computer literate society. In these educational developments the teaching mantle will fall, or should fall, on reading teachers to shoulder the load, for they are already able to interpret reading in terms of the ability of students to process information. It is not therefore just a question of tolerating the machine but one of welcoming it and using it.

The second fundamental point follows from the acceptance of this position. If computers have come to stay and reading teachers are responsible, it becomes imperative that the machine is used for genuine educational purposes. And here two further points arise: the present dearth of good software and, coupled with this, the lack of programs that involve the computer as a tutee. This point is made by Anderson (1984a) who points out that '95% of commercially available computer software in reading and language is the sort where the student is drilled, taught or managed by the computer'. It is vital that students should be allowed to play a more actively creative part in learning.

Textlinguistics

The other force I suggested that would influence our thinking about reading was of a totally different kind, its origin being academic rather than technological. Probably because of this, it is only slowly coming to the fore. It is nevertheless beginning to have its effects as it receives increasing attention from the research community.

Where reading is concerned, textlinguistics, as I've mentioned elsewhere

(Chapman, 1979b) is best thought of as a domain of study that encompasses other disciplines, psychology and sociology as well as linguistics. However, central to the linguistics of the eighties is the movement to describe larger units of text than the sentence. Prominent among those who have drawn attention to these larger units and the interconnectivity involved, is Michael Halliday and his wife Ruqaiya Hasan. Their seminal work, *Cohesion in English*, appeared in 1976 (Halliday and Hasan, 1976) followed by *Text and Context* in 1980 (Halliday and Hasan, 1980). This year sees the publication of *An Introduction to Functional Grammar*, (Halliday, in press).

The cohesion concept has been used widely since its inception and found, in particular, to have significant educational implications. Many papers have been presented to U.K.R.A. Conferences for teachers of reading, reporting research that attempts to define its place in the teaching of reading and the related skills (e.g. Anderson, 1983b; Chapman, 1979a, 1981a, 1981b, 1982, 1983 and 1984). These papers have begun to show the place of cohesion within reading development. As cohesion has been so much the focus of attention it is probably timely to note again that it is one factor of what Halliday has called the 'text-forming component of the semantic system' (Halliday, 1978). In other words it is part of a system of systems which makes up our language capability; it is not an isolated concept.

Cohesion and the microcomputer

Cohesion is a textlinguistic factor that is to do with the interconnectivity found in texts. It has been suggested that without that interconnectivity a text would not be a text. Interconnectivity comes to the fore particularly during the dynamic process of reading. And, because reading is dynamic, the eye continually moving across and down the page, the microcomputer can be aligned to it in a way that is quite new. We have not had the capability of almost instantaneous reaction before.

The cohesive ties, as the cohesive devices are called, are said to occur in patterns through a text and the effects of these patterned interconnections can be illustrated very effectively on a computer screen. Take the small text that was used to demonstrate this phenomenon at the seventeenth U.K.R.A. Conference (Chapman, 1980). Here, because the text is so simple, the chaining of the cohesive ties can be shown clearly as in Figure 1.

In this printed version the text appears inert, but on the computer screen the dynamics involved during reading can be simulated. Each sentence can, for example, be presented with the cohesive tie elements in colour. With the graphics capability of a machine such as the B.B.C. Model B, the key elements can be connected as the presentation proceeds. It is not difficult to imagine how this can be harnessed into very useful prediction activities. Having begun to read, the text is presented line by line, and the reader having encountered the onset of a cohesive tie will be required to predict the other end of the tie not yet visible. This can be accomplished quite simply by leaving the crucial word or words as blank(s). The reader is now asked to replace the word

Figure 1: Cohesive ties: examples of reference, conjunction and lexical cohesion

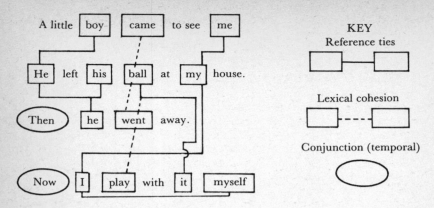

Source: L. J. Chapman (1981b)

or words and having made his or her choice the computer will 'fill in' the pattern to that point if the choice is correct or give indications if not.

Many variations can be made using this basic format, more intricate patterns, different levels and types of texts can be employed. Children can work in pairs, in groups or individually. A further engaging example bringing out the influence of lexical cohesion that has already been experimented with on a microcomputer, can be found in Anderson (1983a).

That these factors are easy to demonstrate arises because the microcomputer combines so readily with our growing understanding of texts and reading. Its versatility is such that Anderson (1984a) was able to give some 20 different uses for reading and language teaching. Each of these can be used imaginatively to considerable effect. If I were asked to single out one of importance I believe the capability of word processing is probably the most significant. This is particularly so in primary schools where there is so much physical energy expended in writing. Also, however careful the child may be, the finished product will be nowhere as satisfying as a printed version. The changes that can be made in drafting, moving whole lines or chunks of text from one place to another, are so easy as to create a willingness on the part of the child to revise and make better. In these tasks, given a knowledge of the cohesive properties of texts as illustrated simply in Figure 1, children can check for connectivity very effectively. Indeed the microcomputer seems almost to have been invented with cohesion in mind for the busy classroom teacher of reading.

References

ANDERSON, J. (1983a) 'Comprehensibility, cohesion and comprehending: procedures for teachers', in J. Anderson and K. Lovett (eds), *Teaching Reading and Writing to Every Child*. Adelaide, S. Australia: Australian Reading Association.

ANDERSON, J. (1983b) 'The writer, the reader and the text', in B. Gillham (ed) *Reading Through the Curriculum*. London: Heinemann Educational.

ANDERSON, J. (1984a) 'The computer as tutor, tutee, tool in reading and language'. *Reading* 18 (2), pp.67–78.

ANDERSON, J. (1984b) 'Reading and technology: the challenge of the chip'. Paper presented at the 10th Australian Reading Conference, Melbourne, August/September 1984.

CHAPMAN, L. J. (1979a) 'Pedagogical strategies for fluent reading', in D. Thackray (ed) *Growth in Reading*. London: Ward Lock.

CHAPMAN, L. J. (1979b) 'Some developments in textlinguistics: implications for the teaching of reading'. Paper read at the Anglo-Scandinavian Conference, Leeds Polytechnic, ERIC 173 767, April.

CHAPMAN, L. J. (1980) 'Reading: prospects for the eighties', in T. Bessell-Browne, R. Latham, N. Reeves and E. Gardiner (eds) *Reading Into the 80's*. Adelaide, S. Australia: Australian Reading Association.

CHAPMAN, L. J. (1981a) 'The importance of the notion of cohesion for teachers of reading'. Paper presented at the 18th Annual Conference of the United Kingdom Reading Association, Edinburgh.

CHAPMAN, L. J. (1981b) 'The reader and the text', in L. J. Chapman (ed) *The Reader and the Text*. London: Heinemann.

CHAPMAN, L. J. (1982) 'Cohesion: an overview'. Paper presented at a symposium on Cohesion, its Measurement and Pedagogy at 9th World Reading Congress of the International Reading Association, Dublin, Ireland. Revised article in *Australian Journal of Reading*, 6(1), March 1983, pp.5–11.

CHAPMAN, L. J. (1983) *Reading Development and Cohesion*. London: Heinemann.

CHAPMAN, L. J. (1984) 'Nurturing every child's literacy development: a four-pronged teaching strategy', in D. Dennis (ed) *Reading: Meeting Children's Special Needs*. London: Heinemann.

HALLIDAY, M. A. K. (1978) *Language as Social Semiotic*. London: Edward Arnold.

HALLIDAY, M. A. K. and HASAN, R. (1976) *Cohesion in English*. Harlow: Longman.

HALLIDAY, M. A. K. and HASAN, R. (1980) *Text and Context*, Working Papers in Linguistics, 6. Tokyo: Sophia University.

HALLIDAY, M. A. K. (in press) *An Introduction to Functional Grammar*. London: Edward Arnold.

McSHANE, R. (1983) 'The history of information processing', *Classroom Computing*, 3(1), pp.2–15.

NAISBITT, J. (1984) *Megatrends*, New York: Warner.

11   Evidence of the cognitive and meta-cognitive effects of punctuation and intonation: can the new technologies help?

Rona F. Flippo

This paper briefly summarises the research and literature relevant to investigating the effects of punctuation and other phrase boundaries, in prose and expository materials, on the intonation and resulting comprehension efforts of children.[1] Additionally, this paper will address the question, 'Is there evidence in the reviewed literature that the new technologies could have an impact on helping children improve their comprehension of text?' Where evidence exists, suggestions for use of the new technologies, based on the reviewed research and literature, are made.[2]

Summary of the research and literature

The literature and research have shown syntax, which includes intonation, to be a developmental process. Intonation miscues can be caused because the reader anticipates the punctuation, or because the reader is unfamiliar with the author's punctuation or structure. For the purpose of this paper, intonation miscues will be defined as those that involve changes in pitch, stress, or pause from what is expected. An initial intonation miscue caused by confusion over punctuation or structure will frequently cause surrounding text items to change their grammatical function. Unexpected punctuation can change grammatic structure and change the meaning of a passage.

The literature and research relevant to the location of punctuation in text has provided some evidence to suggest that modified terminal punctuation should be used for less proficient developing readers (Gutknecht, Apol and Morton, 1982). These readers benefit from terminal punctuation cues at the end of lines of text, rather than those appearing randomly in the text. Punctuation should be used to determine the boundaries between chunks of texts or pausal units (Carver, 1970).

The literature relevant to phrasing of text indicates that text should be printed in meaningful units to facilitate school children's reading comprehension (Weiss, 1983; Raban, 1982; O'Shea and Sindelar, 1983; Cromer, 1970; Stevens, 1981; Carver, 1970). Chunked text should not be broken due to lack of space at right margins (Carver, 1970). Line breaks should be made between phrases, if at all possible, or towards the end of sentences (Raban, 1982). Finally, sentences causing confused intonation should be eliminated from textual materials for young children (Coady and Baldwin, 1977).

Since young developing readers are affected by confusion over intonation, some information should be given to teachers, in the teachers' manuals that accompany the children's readers, for dealing with intonation of text (Coady and Baldwin, 1977).

Goodman and Burke's miscue analysis (1972) gives insight into how children regress and look back to fix up inconsistencies produced while reading, and highlights children's use of syntactic and semantic features. Research information on how children are affected by text structure, such as the information summarised in this paper, coupled with factors of intellect, language background and ability, and physical and emotional stability, allow children to make the most of the events and situations that enhance the transfer of learning. Teachers and publishers should become more aware of the importance that punctuation, intonation, and phrase boundaries have in children's reading comprehension. If text segmentation or end of line punctuation is related to an improvement in developing children's reading comprehension, it might be worthwhile to redesign some texts. It might also be worth the time it takes teachers to redesign instructional stategies to work with children who are still unsophisticated readers on development of strategies to deal more effectively with phrasing, text segmentation, punctuation, and intonation.

Can the new technologies help?

The reviewed literature and research indicate that, for young unsophisticated beginning readers and low ability readers, intonation and resulting comprehension is often affected by punctuation and other phrase boundaries in text. It is possible that the new technologies could have an impact on assisting these readers with comprehension efforts. For instance, use of language experience techniques with a word processor could make children more aware of sentence structure, word groupings, phrase boundaries, and terminal punctuation. Also, voice activators and voice synthesizers could provide cues for intonation. Use of these components might make for an interesting research study in the area under consideration, as well as shed more light on this previously neglected area.

Word processing can be structured to attend to the Gutknecht *et al.* (1982) findings. Beginning readers could be shown the 'word wrap' capability of computer programs. Materials could be more easily rewritten and programmed so that the ending punctuation could be placed at the end of the line of text (Gutknecht *et al.*, 1982; Flippo, 1980, 1982) and line breaks and phrasing could be put in appropriate chunks and locations (Carver, 1970; Raban, 1982; and others). Additionally the word processor could be used to prepare materials for miscue analysis. This would facilitate easier use of miscue analysis in teacher and reading education. The study of miscue analysis could enhance teachers' understanding of punctuation, intonation, and other textual cues and miscues that affect cognition. As pointed out by Coady and Baldwin (1977), the teachers' manuals do not attend to information pertaining to intonation miscues.

Most of the summarised research and literature findings could be facilitated in the classroom by use of a word processor. Microcomputers software could also be developed by reading researchers to enhance the intonation and comprehension success of beginning and less able readers, and this software could be made available for classroom use. Very little is available at this time that could be endorsed. Marsh (1983) suggests that one of the most pressing needs in the microcomputer market is the development of quality software by reading experts. Perhaps use could be made of these summarised research findings, to develop software to assist the unsophisticated reader experiencing difficulty due to problems with location of punctuation, line breaks, and other phrase boundaries?

Notes

1. For a complete and current review of the literature and research, please refer to 'Implication for text design: should phrase boundaries, line breaks and other cues be considered?' (Flippo, 1984, under review). This 1984 review is an update of earlier reviews (Flippo, 1980, 1982). The update was made possible by the work of Hazel Campbell (1984), one of my graduate students, who carried out the update under my guidance and direction.
2. Some of the evidence of technological implications in the reviewed literature and research were from the paper by Hazel Campbell (1984) 'Prosodic, structural and technological influences in reading comprehension', a paper written under my guidance and direction.

References

CAMPBELL, H. (1984) 'Prosodic, structural and technological influences in reading comprehension'. Unpublished paper.

CARVER, R. P. (1970) 'Effect of "chunked" typography on reading rate and comprehension'. *Journal of Applied Psychology*, 54(3), pp.288–96.

COADY, J. and BALDWIN, S. (1977) 'Intonation and syntax in primers'. *Reading Improvements*, 14(3), pp.160–64.

CROMER, W. (1970) 'The difference model: a new explanation for some reading difficulties'. *Journal of Educational Psychology*, 61(6), pp.471–83.

FLIPPO, R. F. (1980) 'The effects of the punctuation/textbook structure on the reading comprehension of elementary grade children'. Proposal for grant submitted to the Teaching and Learning Research Grants Competition, National Institute of Education, Department of Health, Education and Welfare, Washington, D.C.

FLIPPO, R. F. (1982) 'The location of punctuation in the text and its effect on the comprehension of beginning readers: a position paper'. Unpublished manuscript.

FLIPPO, R. F. (1984) 'Implications for text design: should phrase boundaries, line breaks and other cues be considered?' Manuscript under review.

GOODMAN, Y. M. and BURKE, C. L. (1972) *Reading Miscue Inventory manual: Procedure for Diagnosis and Evaluation*. New York: Macmillan.

GUTKNECHT, B., APOL, M. and MORTON, W. (1982) 'Is what you see, what you get?' Paper presented at Florida State Reading Conference, Miami Beach, Fla.

MARSH, M. (1983) 'Computer assisted instruction in reading'. *Journal of Reading*, 26(8), pp.697–701.

O'SHEA, L. J. and SINDELAR, P. T. (1983) 'The effects of segmenting written discourse on reading comprehension of low and high-performance readers'. *Reading Research Quarterly*, 18(4), pp.458–65.

RABAN, B. (1982) 'Text display effects on the fluency of young readers'. *Journal of Research in Reading*, 5(1), pp.7–27.

STEVENS, K. C. (1981) 'Chunking material as an aid to reading comprehension'. *Journal of Reading*, 25(2), pp.126–9.

WEISS, D. S. (1983) 'The effects of text segmentation on children's reading comprehension'. *Discourse Processes*, 6(1), pp.77–89.

Part III: Practice

12   Reading, writing and learning with microcomputers

Jonathan Anderson

How useful is the microcomputer as a stimulus for language in the classroom? Can computers help with reading, writing and learning? What do young children think computers are and how do they react to them? It was these kinds of question which prompted a series of explorations and trials to be reported here.

Described first is a small-scale project conducted with young students in one school (the Teddy Bear Project). The rest of the paper details some newly developed computer software which allows older students to engage in analysis of text in novel and exciting ways.

The Teddy Bear Project

To try to answer at least some of the questions posed above, one approach that suggested itself was to find children who had had no previous experience of computers, introduce microcomputers as part of the regular reading and language programme and, by comparing the children's knowledge and attitudes to this new mode of learning before and after the trial, obtain objective data on the impact of microcomputers in the classroom. This then was the general plan.

Because of the increasing presence of microcomputers, arcade and TV-type games, we thought that if there were any students with little or no knowledge of what a computer was, they would most likely be found in the lower primary levels of school. An approach to one school willing to participate in the study seemed promising. To the school's knowledge, the members of one second-year class had had no formal contact with microcomputers before; neither had the class teacher and there were no microcomputers yet in the school. We thought we had found the subjects we were looking for: a computer-naïve group of children. We were to be proved wrong in this assumption, and probably when the trial was conducted (the middle of 1983) there were few, if any, complete classes in Australian metropolitan schools where this condition was met.

Aims and teaching materials

In the trial to be reported here, there were four broad aims:

(1)   to explore ways of introducing computers in the classroom;
(2)   to use the computer as one component in a reading/language sequence;
(3)   to evaluate pupils' attitudes to computers; and
(4)   to gauge pupils' knowledge of computers following the teaching sequence.

Space does not allow a full description of all aspects of the project. The focus here is on what young children thought about microcomputers and learning with them. A video captures more effectively than words the fun and excitement the children experienced.

Because we wanted to introduce computers in as natural a way as possible, as just another classroom resource, the teaching content was selected first and some computer-related activities were then devised to form part of this language teaching sequence. Adopting an idea of Modla (1983), the topic chosen was to differentiate fact from opinion. Such a topic can be taught at many different levels; it is an important aspect of reading and, for this particular second-year class, it was new. Again following Modla, teddy bears with their wide appeal to young children were chosen as a unifying theme and because they provided an easy way to introduce differences between statements of fact and opinions. Hence the name, the Teddy Bear Project.

The project lasted five weeks. Most of the teaching took place in the first hour of each school day which was usually devoted to reading activities. With the help of a research assistant many teaching materials and activities were developed. These included more than 20 general activities (for example, making bear books, Pooh's crossword, honey pot facts and opinions, a visit to the zoo and, of course, a teddy bears' picnic), as well as specific computer activities. These latter comprised:

(1)   Programs to teach use of the keyboard
      (a) 'Apple Presents . . . Apple' (Apple Computer, 1982)
      (b) 'Introduction to Microcomputers' (Haugo, 1982)
      These are both commercially available programs, their purpose being essentially to familiarise users with the Apple IIe keyboard.

(2)   Programs to reinforce differences between fact and opinion
      (a) 'The Opinion Game'
      (b) 'Fact and Opinion'
      These two programs were adapted from Modla (1983) for the project. Each is designed to reinforce differences between fact and opinion.

(3)   Allied computer activities.
      (a) 'Fun'
      (b) 'Love'
      These two computer activities, illustrated on the following pages, are pure nonsense. They do, however, provide interaction with the computer demonstrating some of its further capabilities such as, for example, to provide printed copy.

```
CHOOSE FUN MESSAGE

1. TEDDY BEARS ARE FUN

2. MY BEAR IS BEST

3. I LOVE TEDDY BEARS

   TYPE 1, 2 OR 3
                TEDDY
                  BEARS
                     ARE FUN
                        TEDDY
                          BEARS
                            ARE FUN
                          TEDDY
                          BEARS
                          ARE FUN
                        TEDDY
                      BEARS
                    ARE FUN
                  TEDDY
              BEARS
          ARE FUN
      TEDDY
    BEARS
  ARE FUN
TEDDY
BEARS
ARE FUN
  TEDDY
    BEARS
        ARE FUN
           TEDDY
              BEARS
                 ARE FUN
                   TEDDY
                     BEARS
                        ARE FUN
                          TEDDY
                          BEARS
                          ARE FUN
                          TEDDY
                        BEARS
                      ARE FUN
                    TEDDY
                BEARS
            ARE FUN
```

```
I  LOVE MY  BEAR I  LOVE  MY  BEAR I  LOVE  MY  BEAR I  LOVE  MY  BEAR
I             R I  LOVE  MY  BEAR I  LOVE  MY            OVE  MY  BEAR
I  L         EAR I  LOVE  MY  BEAR I  LOV                     MY  BEAR
I  LO         BEAR I  LOVE  MY  BEAR I  L                          BEAR
I  LO         BEAR I  LOVE  MY  BEAR I                             BEAR
I  LO         BEAR I  LOVE  MY  BEAR I               AR I  LOV      EAR
I  LO         BEAR I  LOVE  MY  BEAR I               EAR I  LOVE    EAR
I  LO         BEAR I  LOVE  MY  BEAR I               BEAR I  LOVE   EAR
I  LO         BEAR I  LOVE  MY  BEAR I               BEAR I  LOV    EAR
I  LO         BEAR I  LOVE  MY  BEAR I          Y  BEAR I  LO       EAR
I  LO         BEAR I  LOVE  MY  BEAR I         MY  BEAR I  L        EAR
I  LO         BEAR I  LOVE  MY  BEAR I         MY  BEAR I           EAR
I  LO         BEAR I  LOVE  MY  BEAR I         MY  BEAR I           EAR
I  LO         BEAR I  LOVE  MY  BEA  I         MY  BEAR             EAR
I  LO         BEAR I  LOVE  MY  BE   I         MY  BEA              EAR
I  LO         BEAR I  LOVE  MY       I          Y  BEA             EAR
I                             I  LOV              MY  BEAR
I                             I  LOVE MY          OVE  MY  BEAR
I                  I  LO
I                  I  LO
I  LO         BEAR I  LOVE M      EAR I  LOVE       AR I  LOVE MY
I  LOV        EAR I  LOVE        BEAR I  LOVE       AR I  LOVE MY  B
I  LOV        EAR I  LOVE        BEAR I  LOVE       AR I  LOVE MY  BE
I  LOVE        AR I  LOVE        BEAR I  LOVE       AR I  LOVE MY  BEA
I  LOVE        AR I  LOVE        BEAR I  LOVE       AR I  LO E MY  BEAR
I  LOVE        R I  LOV     Y  BEAR I  LOVE         AR I  L    E MY  BEAR
I  LOVE        R I  LOV     Y  BEAR I  LOVE              E MY  BEAR
I  LOVE M         I  LO    MY  BEAR I  LOVE         AR I  L    E MY  BEAR
I  LOVE M         I  LO    MY  BEAR I  LOVE         AR I  LO E MY  BEAR
I  LOVE MY        I  L     MY  BEAR I  LOVE         AR I  LOVE MY  BEA
I  LOVE MY        I  L     MY  BEAR I  LOVE         AR I  LOVE MY  BE
I  LOVE MY             E MY  BEAR I  LOVE           AR I  LOVE MY  B
I  LOVE MY             E MY  BEAR I  LOVE           AR I  LOVE MY
I  LOVE MY  B        VE MY  BEAR I
I  LOVE MY  B        VE MY  BEAR I
I  LOVE MY  BEAR I  LOVE  MY  BEAR I  LOVE MY  BEAR I  LOVE  MY  BEAR
```

Excerpts of the 'Fun' and 'Love' computer programs are illustrated briefly above. The 'Fun' program, for instance, allowed children to select one of three messages which then scrolled down the screen like a twisting snake (actually a rotated sine curve).

With the 'Love' program children made up their own messages about bears and these were printed on paper, to colour in and take home. One example is shown here.

Students' attitudes to computers

We had looked for pupils with no formal exposure to computers in the expectation that student attitudes to learning with these machines would be relatively neutral. This would then allow for movement of attitudes since the project allowed only a very brief introduction and exposure to computers. To check students' contact with computers, information was obtained first from the home. It came as something of a surprise to the teaching staff what computer resources were revealed in parents' replies. It transpired that of the class of 24 pupils:

2 homes had Vic 20s;
7 homes had computer-TV games;
8 parents had computer-related jobs;
5 parents regularly brought computer paper home;
5 families had remembered some discussion about computers.

Only 10 of the pupils – less than half – were judged to have had no prior contact of any kind. There is an implication here for schools which see computer awareness as one of the major tasks.

Obviously, our second-year class had some knowledge and experience of computers even though this had not been gained at school. What did they think computers were and what were their attitudes towards them? A search of the literature found few attitude measures towards computers and none satisfactory for this age level. Accordingly, a short scale was devised (reproduced at the end of this paper). This was administered individually at the start of the project and again following the teaching sequence. Reponses were taped but the sessions were friendly and entirely non-threatening.

Here are responses to a few of the Yes/No items from the group of 24 students, before and after the teaching sequence:

		Before	After
2	have you ever seen a computer?	Yes – 21	Yes – 24

		Before	After
3	Do you know how to use a computer?	Yes – 9	Yes – 23

Clearly there was some movement between the two interviews, which were approximately four weeks apart, though it could not necessarily be assumed that children knew what computers were. Hence, responses to the next question were of interest.

		Before	After
4	Do you think a computer is a bit like:		
	. . . a car	Yes – 2	Yes – 4
	. . . an aeroplane	Yes – 2	Yes – 3
	. . . a radio	Yes – 18	Yes – 7
	. . . a telephone	Yes – 6	Yes – 5
	. . . a typewriter	Yes – 12	Yes – 21
	. . . a television	Yes – 12	Yes – 18

Again, a shift to increased awareness of what a computer is, was evident. There was also a slight shift with regard to confidence about using computers, though being children there was no real shortage of confidence at the start:

		Before	After
7	Do you think that children could use computers?	Yes – 18	Yes – 23

Feelings towards computers again showed a positive shift in attitudes, although most children had quite positive attitudes at the outset:

		Before	After
9	Do you think using computers would be boring?	No – 21	No – 24
10	Do you think computers are friendly?	Yes – 16	Yes – 22
11	Do you think using computers would be fun?	Yes – 24	Yes – 23
12	Would you be scared of a computer?	No – 24	No – 24

The relationship of computers to learning was partly tested with the following item:

		Before	After
16	Do you think computers could help you learn?	Yes – 15	Yes – 23

Discussion

Not discussed above was the enormous enthusiasm generated by the project. No doubt some of this was Hawthorn effect and most the natural zest of young children towards learning of all kinds. Also, teddy bears had been selected because most children like animals and especially teddies (all but one child had at least one teddy bear and even the class teacher had an old favourite). Notwithstanding all of this, the Apple microcomputer itself created a great deal of excitement and each day children enjoyed setting it up in the small withdrawal room. In this way all soon learned about disk drives, floppy disks, monitors and other components of the system.

The development of an attitude scale was an attempt to gauge what students thought computers were and what they felt about them. Although we were not successful in finding a completely computer-naïve group of children, it was clear that attitudes towards computers, even by students with little or no prior contact, were positive. And short though the project was, attitudes moved to being even more positive. No statistics were computed because the trends are so clear. Nevertheless, there are some observations that deserve comment and perhaps merit further investigation.

Readers will have noticed that when asked whether using a computer would be fun, one child, who had previously thought it might, changed his mind following the trial. Some of the computer activities were of the drill and practice kind and his response ('Not really that much – but it is when you play games') possibly reflected this.

Another trend worth noting, though not part of the design of the study, is the responses of boys and girls. In our class of 24 there were, as it happened, 12 boys and 12 girls. Of the five children who said at the beginning that they did not think computers were friendly, all were girls (the remaining three not responding 'Yes', one girl and two boys, responded 'Don't know'). Even after the trial, when 22 children responded that they thought computers were friendly, the remaining two were girls who had not changed their minds. This observation may of course be a function of the particular group but, if tested for statistical significance, it would surely be highly significant.

New kinds of reading software

Microcomputers can do much more than merely drill students. They can be powerful aids in the classroom for reading, writing and learning (see, for example, Chandler, 1983; Anderson, 1984a, where such application as word processing, simulations and information retrieval are described). The important proviso is that teachers have access to appropriate software and are confident about its use. At the same time new kinds of software are being developed which offer the promise, at least, of ushering in different modes of learning.

There is a need to disseminate information about these newer programs and to trial them in the classroom. To meet this first need, some further ways are now described of using this most versatile of machines – the microcomputer – in the classroom, to enhance language learning.

Text-based games

The following program is one example of an activity that might have application in the reading language classroom.

Title	: 'Word Search'
Publishers	: Elizabeth Computer Centre
Date	: 1984
Suitable for	: All levels
Instructional mode	: Educational game
System requirements	: B.B.C. Model B/Disk/32k
Contents	: Disk and manual
Cost	: Unknown
Available from	: Elizabeth Computer Centre
	Cnr Warwick & Murray St.
	Hobart, Tas 7000

Publisher's description: ' . . . a program designed to develop language skills. A piece of text is stored in the computer but remains hidden from students. The letters which make up each word are shown with + signs . . . there is a great deal of flexibility with regard to how much guessing students will have to undertake. It has applications in primary and secondary schools, the level of difficulty being totally dependent on the text which is selected.'

One of the strong features of this program is a built-in editor which allows teachers to add their own stories. This is a feature I rate highly in computer software since it is highly unlikely that learning materials chosen by others are going to meet precisely my needs, or those of my students.

One fairly obvious application of 'Word Search' is as a cloze activity. In the following example, words have been deleted regularly through the passage though the teacher has complete control over which parts of the text are shown and which parts are hidden:

Paper is so common today that it + + difficult to think that many years ago + + was an important invention. About four thousand + + + + ago the Egyptians first made a paperlike + + + + + + +. They made it from the stems of + + + papyrus plants that grew along the Nile + + + + +.

In this program students are invited to guess the missing words, and this they may do in any order. If they are correct, the plus signs are replaced and a record is shown of the number of words filled and the number still to be found. As with many other computer activities, much incidental learning results from students' working together in small groups.

Yet another possibility is to use 'Word Search' as a measure of textual cohesion, illustrated in the following excerpt, an interesting passage discussed in more detail elsewhere (Anderson 1983):

1 They knew that old Violet was going to die.
2 So it was no surprise when + + + did.
3 She left her perch on Tuesday at noon, and lay down on her side at the bottom of the cage.
4 She rested that way for the next three days.
5 On Friday morning Amy and Eva said good-bye for the last time.
6 The funeral was held on Saturday morning.
7 Close friends and neighbours were invited.
8 Billy came.
9 He brought the box.
10 Elizabeth + + + + to the funeral too.
11 She brought a ribbon to tie around the + + +.
12 She also + + + + + + + her little brother Danny.
13 They were very dear and old friends of the + + + +.

To replace the first blank, students must perceive the cohesive tie with 'Violet' in the preceding sentence. It is such cohesive ties that bind text together, in fact make 'a text a text' according to Halliday and Hasan (1976). There is evidence that the perception of these cohesive ties is a major component of reading comprehension with native English speakers (Chapman, 1983) and also with Italian and Punjabi speakers for whom English is a second language (Anderson, 1982).

When students enter the pronoun 'she' an interesting feature of the program (possibly one not intended by the authors) is for the word to be inserted in the text in a different colour, and at the same time the other instances of the pronoun 'she' in succeeding sentences also change colour. In this way the cohesive chain, or thread running through the text, is clearly demonstrated. Similarly, when 'came', 'box' and 'brought' are entered as replacements in sentences 10, 11 and 12, the cohesive chains binding the text are shown on the screen.

Processing text

In a recent overview of microcomputers in reading (Anderson 1984a), I described a computer program, 'Tray', being produced as part of M.E.P. The name derives from the way a picture slowly emerges in a photographer's developing tray. So, similarly, this program requires text that is initially hidden to be developed by readers. Another writer (Govier, 1983) described the program as creating 'a new dynamic approach to the teaching of reading' (p.46); the processes called for in this computer activity, she continued, require 'the simultaneous application of analytic, convergent thinking as well as creative thought' (p.49). The game certainly links reading, writing and thinking.

A somewhat similar program called 'Passage', just released in Australia, is proving to have many useful applications, not only for English classes but in the teaching of foreign languages as well.

Title	:	'Passage'
Publishers	:	Elizabeth Computer Centre
Date	:	1984
Suitable for	:	All levels
Instructional mode	:	Educational game
System requirements	:	B.B.C. Model B/Disk/32k
Contents	:	Disk and manual
Cost	:	Unknown
Available from	:	Elizabeth Computer Centre
		Cnr Warwick & Murray St.
		Hobart, Tas 7000

Publisher's description:' . . . a program designed for use in English, social science and language classes. It . . . uses the computer's facility for gradual revelation of visual information. The goal is to fill in a passage of writing which is slowly built up on the screen . . . The sessions require absolute concentration and stimulate group discussion over which letter to buy, where to place parts of words, and the eventual meaning of the piece of writing.'

As in the previous program, short texts may be entered by teachers. Initially, all that is displayed are punctuation marks, the students' task being to 'develop' the text by judicious guessing of letters.

Much learning about language generally results – for example, learning about the probabilities of occurrence of letters singly, of digraphs and, as the text is progressively displayed, of phrases and of words. It is not an easy task, so be warned. Nevertheless, the game format of buying letters of the alphabet, working in groups, making hypotheses, to have these confirmed or rejected as the text is slowly revealed, is quite an enjoyable experience. It is certainly a new approach to teaching reading comprehension and one that merits the attention of all reading teachers.

Concluding note

The use of microcomputers in the classroom is a relatively recent phenomenon. Prior to 1983 their use, at least in Australian schools, was not widespread (Sandery, 1982). Yet in the trial reported here, we were not able to find an entire class of pupils which had not, in some way, been affected by the advent of the microprocessor. The introduction of micros into the classroom has been rapid and pervasive.

Students clearly accept microcomputers very readily, just as they accept all new experiences. The Teddy Bear Project was an attempt to gauge students' attitudes towards computers. Within the limitations of this small school-based project, it was evident that feelings towards this new classroom resource are most favourable.

The microcomputer can undoubtedly be a powerful and effective force for language learning. All too frequently, though, computer programs are promoted as educational when they are little more than electronic worksheets and, in fact, run counter to the philosophy of reading held by many teachers. Hence the claim that much presently available software is disappointing and, worse, is bad. On the other hand, there is some excellent software becoming available which may change the very nature of the curriculum.

References

ANDERSON, J. (1982) 'The measurement of the perception of cohesion: a second language example'. Paper presented to the Ninth World Congress of Reading, Dublin (ED 222 885).

ANDERSON, J. (1983) 'Comprehensibility, cohesion and comprehending: procedures for teachers', in J. Anderson and K. Lovett (eds) *Teaching Reading and Writing to Every Child*. Adelaide: Australian Reading Association.

ANDERSON, J. (1984a) 'The computer as tutor, tutee, tool in reading and language'. *Reading*, 18.

ANDERSON, J. (1984b) *Computing in Schools: An Australian Perspective*. Melbourne: Australian Council for Educational Research.

APPLE COMPUTER (1982) *Apple presents . . . . Apple* (An Introduction to the Apple IIe Computer). Cupertino: Apple Computer.

CHANDLER, D. (ed) (1983) *Exploring English with Microcomputers*. Leicester: Council for Educational Technology.

CHAPMAN, J. (1983) 'Cohesion: an overview'. *Australian Journal of Reading*, 6, pp.5–11.

GOVIER, H. (1983) 'Primary language development'. *Acorn User*, 10, pp.45–51.

HALLIDAY, M. A. K. and HASAN, R. (1976) *Cohesion in English*. Harlow: Longman.

HAUGO, J. (1982) *Introduction to Microcomputers* (for the Apple). New York: McGraw-Hill.

MODLA, V. B. (1983) 'Writing a software program to improve reading comprehension – a step by step procedure'. Paper presented to 28th Annual Convention of the International Reading Association, Anaheim, Calif.

SANDERY, P. (1982) *The Future Role of Computers in Education*. Sydney: Institute of Public Affairs (New South Wales).

ATTITUDES TO COMPUTERS

Informal Interview for Young Children[1]

Name:_____ Grade:_____ Date:_____

	YES	NO	DON'T KNOW
1 Have you ever heard of a computer?			
2 Have you ever seen a computer? If YES, where? _____			
Anywhere else? _____			
3 Do you know how to use a computer? If YES: a) How did you learn to use a computer? _____			
b) Do you like using a computer? _____			
c) What do you like using a computer for? _____			
4 Do you think a computer is a bit like			
a car? If YES, how? _____			
an aeroplane? " _____			
a radio? " _____			
a telephone? " _____			
a typewriter? " _____			
a television? " _____			
5 What do you think a computer is? _____			
6 Where do you think you might find computers? _____			
Anywhere else? _____			

	YES	NO	DON'T KNOW
7 Do you think that children could use computers? If NO, why not? _____			
8 Do you think that grownups could use computers? If NO, why not? _____			
Who do you think might use them? _____			
9 Do you think using computers would be boring?			
10 Do you think computers are friendly?			
11 Do you think using computers would be fun?			
12 Would you be scared of a computer? If YES, why? _____			
13 Do you think you would like to use a computer? If YES, what for? _____			
14 Do we need to learn about computers? Why? _____			
15 Do you think computers could be used in schools? If YES, what for? _____			
What else? _____			
16 Do you think computers could help you learn? If YES, what could a computer teach you? _____			
17 What things could your teacher teach you that a computer could not? _____			
18 What things could a computer teach you that your teacher could not? _____			
19 In the classroom do you like working best a) on your own? _____ b) with a friend, or _____ c) in a small group? _____			
20 Your teacher helps you learn. In the classroom what else helps you learn? _____			
Outside the classroom what helps you learn? _____			

[1]This scale may be reproduced for educational purposes with the usual acknowledgement of source (Jonathan Anderson – Flinders University of South Australia).

13   Organising group work with a micro

Sℓℓ Summary

Frank Potter and Steve Walker

While the usefulness of microcomputers will clearly depend upon the quality of the software available, it is also true that the value of the programs themselves will depend upon how they are used. It was with this in mind that we decided to conduct a detailed evaluation of how best to use two programs to develop children's writing. This took the form of a collaboration between an observer and a teacher of third-year juniors. As we have just finished collecting the data, what follows is a brief report of some of the preliminary conclusions we have drawn after using one of the programs. A fuller report is in preparation (Potter, 1984). We have selected those findings which we believe can be most readily generalised to other programs, rather than those which are more 'program-specific'.

The program in question, 'Divergent Cloze', has a clear theoretical rationale, and was devised to encourage children to use the context to help decode unfamiliar words.

A brief description of the program

In this program the children's task is to think of a number of guesses for each gap in a cloze passage (hence divergent cloze). The computer then classifies each guess as GOOD, POOR or POSSIBLE (neither good nor poor), or admits that it does not have sufficient data to classify it (a NEW GUESS). Their guesses are stored for later review by the teacher. The program can trap more than 80 per cent of the children's misspellings. We have described most of the development of this program elsewhere (Walker and Potter, 1984). Since then an additional feature has been added – the children can choose to obtain letter clues (described as 'hints'), which consist of the initial letter blends of the good guesses, together with an indication of the length of the word – e.g. w--- for warm, str---- for stream, etc.

An important feature of the program is that the data (the good guesses, the poor guesses, etc.) are stored in data files. This means that the program can be used with any text, as long as the appropriate data file is created.

The procedure adopted

Originally devised to help teach reading, the program lends itself to the development of children's writing. Good writing includes the ability to choose the most appropriate word, after first considering various alternatives. This is precisely what the program 'Divergent Cloze' encourages. However, in order to develop children's writing, the program needs to be used in a different way. Briefly, the procedure we adopted was as follows.

(1) The children used the program with a selected text.
(2) The children then created their own cloze text and produced their own data.
(3) The children gave their text and program to another group to do.
(4) The other group evaluated the data.
(5) The original group revised their data.

The choice of procedure is explained fully elsewhere (Potter, 1984), but essentially the reasoning is as follows. The children were required to create their own cloze text and revise their data in an attempt to ensure that they saw the relevance of the activity as a way of improving their own writing. The purpose of evaluating another group's data, in the context of the total sequence of activities, was to increase the children's awareness of the status of the computer's judgement – that is, when the computer responds to a particular word by saying that it is a 'good guess', it is only relaying the judgement of the creator of the data file.

Organising the group work

One of our main aims was to investigate the most effective way of organising group work with the programs. We will present our preliminary conclusions concerning the organisation of group work in three sections: explaining the task demands; organising the review; and choosing the group size.

Explaining the task demands

On reflection we now favour a class demonstration of the task as a whole. This has three advantages: it saves teacher time, it is simpler to organise, and it helps children to understand the purpose of the task as a whole.

As the children were working in groups, it seemed only natural to explain the tasks to each group in turn. Each group was shown how to use the program, and told how to complete the worksheet. Whilst only a few minutes were needed to explain the tasks to each group, with up to nine groups involved the total time was significant. Besides, it is wasteful to give the entire explanation to nine groups in turn when it can be better said to the class as a whole.

More significant than the waste of time is the timing of the explanation – the children usually needed to be started off at the same time as the rest of the class were being explained a different task. There are other ways round this problem, such as giving the children another task to do first, but it is simpler if they already know what to do.

Thirdly, the children will have a better idea of the purpose of the task if they have an overview of the task as a whole. For example, we observed that sometimes children were inhibited about entering a guess (in case they were wrong?) – and we think they may have been less inhibited had they known they would be required to evaluate all the guesses later.

Organising the review

Some sort of review was always regarded as essential, as the program can only replace the more routine functions of the teacher, but this review should be distinguished from the 'follow-up' activities.

Originally the computer simply displayed the children's work at the end so that the teacher and children could review the work together. Here again both the time and timing was a problem.

Because the program was so good at directing the children and providing feedback, no teacher intervention was needed and the children worked completely on their own. Paradoxically this meant that it took a significant time for the teacher to 'size up' the situation – to evaluate the children's work in sufficient depth to be able to ask useful questions or make intelligent comments. In addition the children seemed to perceive this as a time for the teacher to take the initiative, and expected the teacher to take on a didactic role.

The timing was again a problem. The children worked through the program extremely well without any teacher intervention, but the review came towards the end of a session, just when the rest of the class began to need more guidance and attention.

Our solution to these problems was to have a break between the program and the review, and to structure the review so that the children could work independently, making it possible for the timing of the teacher intervention to be more flexible. This structure took the form of a worksheet. This solution also gave the teacher the opportunity to look at the children's work at leisure, and outside valuable class time. The children were therefore able to start the review at the beginning of a session, and the teacher could then join them, having already seen their work, when the rest of the children were settled, and before they started meeting problems or finishing their work.

This arrangement was a major improvement, but for it to be possible the children's work has either to be SAVED on cassette or tape, or printed out on paper. The program was modified to enable the teacher to choose either option, but the printout option has two advantages. It means that the computer is not needed for the review stage, and also that the printout can take the form of a worksheet. This enables more efficient use to be made of the computer, saving approximately 40 per cent of computer time, and avoids the need to produce a separate worksheet. The worksheet is slightly superior, in that the data are also printed out. This makes it a clear favourite with the children, who do not need to copy tediously from the screen onto the worksheet.

The only thing that concerned us was whether the delay between the program and the review might result in an inferior review on the part of the children. We therefore compared three different arrangements: one where there was no delay between the program and the review, another where there was a short delay of about 15 minutes (playtime), and a third where there was a delay of about 24 hours.

We found that the longer the delay, the more time and trouble the children took over the review. Our feeling is that the children needed a break because they work so hard when they are using the program, (see Table 1).

Table 1: *Time on task (in minutes) as a function of length of delay between the program and review*

	No delay	Short delay (15 minutes)	Long delay (24 hours)
Mean	11	21	28
Standard deviation	1.4	5.0	4.2
Number of groups	3	3	3

$$F(2,6) = 9.56, \ p < 0.05$$

If all the children are using the same text, an even better method is then possible. During the review the amount of teacher involvement is purposely kept minimal, but a third stage is added – the class exchange. After each group has reviewed the data and completed the worksheet, the groups then 'compare notes' in a class session. This enables differences of opinion to be discussed between peers, and rather than the teacher having to challenge a group to justify their choice, the group's peers do so. Therefore not only does this class exchange enable the teacher's time to be used most efficiently, it also has a significant pedagogical advantage. We were interested to read, only days after coming to this conclusion, what Lunzer and Gardner (1984) had to say in their recent book on 'DARTS' (p.20):

> For all these reasons the preferred pattern of working for all teachers associated with the project has been (1) class introduction, (2) work in small groups, (3) class discussions to exchange ideas, to bring out some key points, and generally to round off the lesson and perhaps set the scene for another.

Choosing the group size

In terms of classroom organisation it would be desirable to be able to have a large group, possibly five or six working on the computer, but the common consensus seems to be that a group of three is the ideal size, and this accords with our impressions from our previous work. With larger groups the children at the ends seem to find it difficult to see the screen and to communicate with the other children.

However this presupposes that the children are seated in a row at a rectangular table – see Figure 1. We experimented with different layouts, and found that as many as five children could be accommodated comfortably (we did not try six), as long as they were seated round a semi-circular table with the monitor set back to allow the angle of vision to be wide enough – see Figure 2. This new layout was clearly preferred by the children. Since the lead supplied with the B.B.C. machine is only one metre long, we needed to have a longer one made up.

We compared children working in groups of three, four and five, to deter-

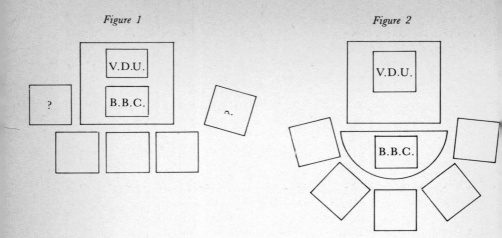

Figure 1   Figure 2

mine the largest satisfactory group size. We expected three to be the optimum
size, but wanted to determine if a larger group was satisfactory, that is,
whether children could be placed in a larger group without any of them being
'left out'. To our surprise, not only was a group of four satisfactory, but it also
turned out to be the optimum size in terms of the amount of task-related talk.
Not only was the total amount of discussion greater than with a group of three,
as would be expected (there being more children), but individual children also
contributed more to the discussion. This is the opposite to what one would
expect, as there is more opportunity to make a contribution in a smaller group
– see Table 2. It seems that children are more likely to 'spark each other off' in
a group of four.

*Table 2: Relative amount of task related talk as a function of group size
(taking group of 3 as the standard = 100)*

| | Average amount of task related talk, relative to group 3 | |
Size of group	(for individuals within groups)	(for groups as a whole)
3	100	100
4	112	150
5	80	133
	$F_{(2,6)} = 5.52$, $p < 0.05$	$F_{(2,6)} = 7.55$ $p < 0.05$

There were nine groups in all, three of each size. The results are presented in this way for clarity's
sake and for brevity. More details can be found in Potter (1984). The children were observed at
five-second intervals in rotation, and it was noted whether they were on or off-task, and whether or
not they were talking.

112

In a group of five the children at the ends made significantly fewer contributions, and there seemed to be significantly less cohesion. Also, it is notable that practically the only instances of off-task behaviour occurred in these groups. For these reasons we feel that these larger groups were not satisfactory. This does not mean that a group of five might not be successful under different circumstances, for example if the children were more used to group work, of if they were given clearly defined roles in the group situation.

To conclude, given the appropriate physical layout, we found that four was the optimum group size. We are fairly confident that this would generalise to many other programs, but not necessarily to all uses of the computer. We have the feeling that the use of a computer as a word processor might be best with groups of three, but then again we could be in for another surprise.

From experience, we would also recommend that the groups should be composed of children of similar ability and the same sex, at least initially.

Summary

To summarise, our work has led us to the following conclusions:

(1)   For more efficient teaching, and more effective learning, there should be a class demonstration of the program and review. This means that the program has to have more than one set of data.

(2)   There should be a delay between work on the computer and the review, to give the children a break and the teacher a chance to look at their work. This means that the children's work has to be saved, either as a data file or printed out on paper. The printout is the best solution, as this then releases the computer for use by another group. Furthermore, the printout can also take the form of a worksheet which the children begin on their own, leaving the timing of the teacher involvement flexible. If all groups are using the same text, then there should be a third stage – the *class exchange*.

(3)   There should be four children in a group, of similar ability and the same sex, seated in an arc around a semi-circular table, with the monitor moved back to enable all children to have a good view. This means getting a longer lead.

Acknowledgements

This research was made possible by the secondment of one of the authors from Edge Hill College of Higher Education to the Centre for Educational Research and Development at Lancaster University. The authors also wish to thank Mr Parkinson, Roy Morgan, Ken Harrison, and John Gidman.

References

LUNZER, E. and GARDNER, K. (1984) *Learning from the Written Word*. Edinburgh: Oliver & Boyd.

113

POTTER, F. N. (1984) Report to the Centre for Educational Research and Development, Lancaster University.

WALKER, S. and POTTER, F. (1984) 'The development of a divergent cloze microcomputer program'. *Reading,* 18, pp.79–88.

14 The adventurous way to use the computer

David Wray

You are in a large cave. The floor is dry although you can hear water trickling somewhere. It is rather gloomy but there is just enough light to see by.

You can go north.

You can see a spear.

What will you do now?

GET SPEAR

O.K. You now have a spear.

What will you do now?

GO NORTH

You are in a deep canyon. The walls are very steep and impossible to climb.

It is very barren here.

You can go North or South.

You can see a fierce tiger.

What will you do now?

The adventure has begun. You have been placed in an imaginary world with only the computer as your eyes and ears. Your destiny is under your own control and you have to negotiate your way through many obstacles and problems before you can solve the adventure, perhaps by finding some hidden treasure or maybe simply by escaping from this dangerous world.

It is easy to see why adventure games are so popular among computer users. They provide enthralling situations in which one's ability to survive is determined not by sheer reactions, as in the familiar arcade-type games, but by the ability to reason logically and, very often, fairly divergently. Playing an adventure game is a bit like reading a thrilling novel, with the vital difference that the sequence of events is not fixed, but is determined by the choices made by the player.

It has been suggested (Wray, 1983; Fawcett, 1983) that adventure games have a great deal of potential in the classroom, especially in terms of the development of reading and language. This paper will attempt to outline some of the possible benefits in terms of the reading and language skills that may be developed.

First and foremost amongst these must come the range of problem-solving skills that players are obliged to employ during the games. At every stage the player is confronted with some kind of problem, some easy enough to solve, but some requiring a great deal of logical reasoning and often inspired deductions. For example, in the adventure 'Philosopher's Quest', the player begins in a shop in which there are four objects on view. As all of these objects are likely to be needed later on to solve other problems, the first reaction is to try to take all four. Unfortunately, as a sign on the wall informs you, you are only allowed to take two of them. If you try to take two out of the shop, drop them and then come back for the other two, you find they have vanished. After a great deal of thought it occurs that there is more than one way of getting the objects out of the shop. It is possible to throw some of them through the door first, and these do not then count as the two objects taken. Outside the door all the objects can be picked up and the player moves on to the next problem.

As another example, in the adventure 'Dinosaur Adventure', the player arrives eventually at a desert which has to be crossed, but in which there is no water supply. Try to cross it without water and you will be told you have died of thirst. It is necessary to backtrack to an earlier point in the game at which there is a running stream. Unfortunately if you try to get water from the stream you are told you have nothing to carry it in. Hidden somewhere else in this inhospitable landscape is a vital jug. Finding it is a further problem.

Linked with the ability to solve problems is the necessity in these games to test out various hypotheses. The question uppermost in most players' minds will be 'What will happen if we do this?', and it may be that some problems have several likely-looking solutions, some of which may, in fact, lead to further problems later on. As an example, in 'Dinosaur Adventure', the player, after negotiating the desert, comes across a caveman carrying an axe. Two possible responses suggest themselves straight away and these are usually tested quite quickly. The first is to kill the caveman with the spear that you are carrying. This unfortunately leads to a swift demise as the caveman is much better with his axe than you are with your spear. The second possible answer is to ignore the caveman and sneak past him. This seems to work fine until you find that later you encounter an impenetrable jungle. To chop a way through this you need, of course, an axe. There has, then, to be a third way past the caveman which will leave you in possession of his axe. Next time around you can try swapping the axe for something you are holding. You will have to test out a few more hypotheses to discover what this is.

Skills which can be developed, and which are concerned more specifically with reading, include those involved in reading very carefully for small details. Reading the descriptions on the screen too quickly and in a careless way may lead to certain vital clues being missed. For example in 'Pirate Adventure', the player quite early in the game comes across several objects which do not immediately seem useful. One of these is a pair of sneakers. They are not just ordinary sneakers, however, as they are described as 'non-slip sneakers'. Very shortly the player will have to stand on the outside window ledge of an apartment, and if not wearing these *non-slip* sneakers, an unsurvivable slip to the road below will result. Adventure games are full of this kind of vital but tiny clue, and would seem to provide a very motivating way of demonstrating to careless readers the importance of noticing small details in their reading.

Another reading skill which can be developed is that of reading between the

116

lines. Several of the descriptions to be found in adventure games are deliberately cryptic and some thought is necessary to understand the implications and hints being given. For example, in 'Adventureland' you are exploring a system of caves, carrying a lighted lamp, when you see a strange scratched message on the wall. It says, 'Aladdin was here'. Some knowledge of fairy stories is necessary to realise that this is a hint to rub your lamp. A genie does appear, although unfortunately he is not quite as useful as Aladdin's genie.

The possibilities for skill development offered by adventure games have so far been described as if the games were purely an activity for individuals. In an educational context it is vital to realise that the major benefit of these activities will be the co-operation and *shared* reading and problem-solving they can engender if they are organised on a group rather than individual basis. To observe a group of three or four children (or adults for that matter) working their way through 'Adventureland', or 'Dinosaur Adventure', is to realise very quickly that in this situation there will be far more interaction between group members than with the computer. The computer will be used as an arbiter of group decisions, but the real learning potential is in the discussion that precedes each of these decisions. In this regard the use of the computer adventure game with a group of children is very similar to the use of other group reading or discussion activities such as cloze and prediction tasks. The children are posed problems by a printed text (either on paper or on the screen) and have to arrive at joint solutions. As with cloze or prediction it is not getting the correct answer which is so important in the learning process, but the discussion and the sharing and justification of possible ideas which precedes suggested solutions.

The last point makes it clear that, as with all teaching activities, the benefit which accrues from adventure games will be determined more by the way in which they are organised and developed by the teacher, than by the activities themselves. This is especially true with regard to the potential of these games to stimulate creative work in a wide variety of curriculum situations. It is fairly obvious to suggest that work on 'Dinosaur Adventure' might stimulate further work on dinosaurs, or that 'Pirate Adventure' might lead to the use of pirates as a creative theme, and, in the latter case especially, some research into pirate ships, and some knowledge of typical story-book pirates will be necessary to solve the adventure. Reports are slowly beginning to appear of the use of this kind of activity in the classroom (Matson 1983). One very valuable use would appear to be as the stimulus for creative thought and writing as groups and individual try, away from the computer, to predict ways in which the adventure might develop during their next turns. As earlier remarked, the imaginative stimulus from a computer adventure game can equal that from a novel, with the added ingredient that the player can actually determine the way in which events unfold.

Having described some of the potential benefits of computer adventure games in a language curriculum, it would be unfair not to mention their biggest weakness. Due to the nature of the computer itself or perhaps, more correctly, to the present state of programming sophistication, although adventure games appear at first sight to be very open-ended, they all do, in fact, have *a* correct solution, and the aim of the player is, ultimately, to discover this solution. There are one or two games at present on the market, such as 'The Hobbit', in which, due to a random factor, the game varies slightly every time it is played. The variation is, however, only slight and the same basic solution always applies. This means that the game can be allowed to become an exercise in convergent thinking, with the players struggling to read the, sometimes extremely idiosyncratic, mind of the program writer. There is no ideally satisfactory answer to this problem, although it is suggested that using the games as stimuli for creative work across the whole curriculum, as earlier described, may counteract it to a large extent. After all, the same phenomenon is present in stories in books. Children may speculate all they will about what will happen to Snow White, and gain much benefit from it, but in the end she still has to eat the apple, and be rescued by Prince Charming!

Computer adventure games do have their weaknesses but it is hoped that enough justification has been put forward in this short paper to suggest that, at the present, primitive stage of development of educational software, they have some potential for the enrichment of many skills and attitudes highly prized in an effective reading and language curriculum.

References

FAWCETT, J. (1983) 'Feeling adventurous'. *Microcomputers* (Greater Manchester Primary Contact, Special Issue Number 2, Manchester Polytechnic), pp.120–22.
MATSON, M. (1983) 'Spacex, a computer-based project'. *Microcomputers* (Greater Manchester Primary Contact, Special Issue Number 2, Manchester Polytechnic), pp.116–19.
WRAY, D. (1983) 'Computer-assisted learning in language and reading'. *Reading*, 17(1).

Adventure games mentioned in text (all available for B.B.C. Model B computer):
 'Philosopher's Quest'. Acornsoft.
 'Dinosaur Adventure'. Available through Prestel Micro-computing, or from author.
 'Pirate Adventure'. Adventure International.
 'Adventureland'. Adventure International.
 'The Hobbit'. Melbourne House.

15   Word processing in the primary classroom

C. Broderick and J. Trushell

The 1980s have seen an increasingly comprehensive international literature on the technological revolution relating to the introduction of the micro-computer into education.

It is still not uncommon, as Frank Potter noted in the proceedings of the 1983 U.K.R.A. Conference, for experienced teachers to be rather sceptical about the use of the new technology in the teaching of language and reading. He points out that:

> It may be that the micro's role will be limited in this area, but on the other hand we may discover a wide range of useful applications. The answer is that we won't know until we have explored and evaluated many different possibilities. (Potter, 1984)

The 'scepticism' which Potter attributes to the teachers' reception of educational innovation, Derek Rowntree interprets as justifiable reluctance:

> 'Yes, but . . . ' is the automatic response to would-be innovators. In view of the hordes of unvalidated fads and fancies with which education is constantly assailed, this stance has some survival value. (Rowntree, 1974)

However, the word processor is neither fad nor fancy but a fact: word processing is simply one application of the revolutionary technology which is rapidly pervading not merely education but every aspect of contemporary society.

As every primary and secondary school in Britain should possess a microcomputer by the end of 1984 – most will have word processor potential and may also have the relevant peripherals of printer and cassette or disk memory – there is a growing need for an examination by teachers of the implications of the new technology and some guidance as to how it will contribute to or indeed change the curriculum.

This paper describes a research project which examined the use of word processing facilities in the primary school and sought to assess the implications for both word processing and writing development.

The initiatives for the project came from staff of the School for Education and Humanities at the North East London Polytechnic (N.E.L.P.) who had previously been involved in observations of children's use of computers and in the study of children's writing processes and products.

It was felt that the use of word processing facilities:

(1)   could make the process of writing more susceptible to study,

(2) could give some emphasis to the drafting and editing aspects of the writing process,

(3) could usefully integrate reading, writing and talking as aspects of the language curriculum, and

(4) might even go some way towards repudiating the charge made by Morley Sage and David J. Smith that 'the teaching profession in the U.K. . . . retains a remarkable propensity for intellectual 'luddism' ' (Sage and Smith, 1983).

The paper is organised in sections relevant to the phases in which the research was conducted.

A survey of current practice

The preliminary phase of the N.E.L.P. research, autumn term 1983, involved a survey of word processing practices in the primary sector, featuring a variety of primary schools in the outer London boroughs and in the Inner London Education Authority, (I.L.E.A.), including several schools participating in the I.L.E.A. Primary Pilot Project.

Children were observed while word processing, either 'fair copying' from script or composing text, both individually and collaboratively.

Observers noted that often children were selected meritoriously for word processing: children whose early drafts had achieved a certain standard were permitted to 'fair copy' on to the word processor. This prevalence of 'fair copying' may be seen as a consequence of the relative scarcity of micro-computers as a classroom resource, a phenomenon noted by Henry Olds in 'Word processing. How will it shape the student as a writer?' (Olds, 1982).

These phenomena were observed in schools where the particular emphasis was upon individual composition in timetabled writing lessons. Elsewhere, there were a few examples of children having greater access to the word processor, either working individually across the timetable or collaboratively in groups of between two and five.

The survey led to the decisions that in the research project:

(1) children should be encouraged to compose text rather than produce 'fair copy' on the word processor.

(2) children should compose collaboratively rather than individually, and

(3) children should have the opportunity to explore every aspect of the word processor facilities.

The word processor program selected particularly for the purposes of the research was 'Wordwise' (Computer Concepts, 1982) for the B.B.C. Model 'B' microcomputer. 'Wordwise' has the advantages of being simple, direct and attractive when compared to other word processing programs.

Moreover, 'Wordwise' is particularly compatible with the word processing peripherals – printer and disk drive – which increases the potential alternatives of presentation and facilitates the manipulation of memorised text.

The research project in school

An east London primary school was chosen for the second phase of the research which was conducted with the entire fourth year. The school had acquired, through the M.E.P./D.O.I. subsidy scheme, a B.B.C. Model B microcomputer without 'Wordwise': thus, while some pupils had had an opportunity for 'hands on' experience of a microcomputer, few pupils had any previous knowledge of word processing.

Once access had been negotiated, conduct of the research became a co-operative venture between the researchers and the headteacher and staff of the school. It was agreed that the 48 fourth-year (10-year-old) pupils were to be released in groups of three, selected by their class teachers, for 40-minute sessions once a week for nine weeks during spring term 1984. The data for the research were to be gathered from the schoolwork that the sample children would normally have undertaken, but with an emphasis on certain aspects of the writing tasks which drew on the word processing facilities.

The pupils were introduced to word processing in the least obtrusive manner possible: as a medium for recording their project work. The first week's sessions were devoted to familiarisation with 'Wordwise', which was accomplished by the completion of two tasks:

(1)   each pupil composed a cover for his/her project folder, featuring his/her name, class and project title, and
(2)   each pupil entered his/her name and address in a register.

While performing these tasks, the pupils entered text, embedded commands and became accustomed to the terms MENU, EDIT MODE, PREVIEW and PRINT. The pupils retained most of these initial skills and a familiarity with the terms until the next week of the project.

The schedule for the remaining eight weeks was as follows:

weeks two to four   – story assignment,
weeks five to six   – poetry assignment,
weeks seven to nine – informational assignment.

These assignments were devised by the researchers and school staff as components of a project on fire prevention, incorporating materials provided by the London Fire Brigade:

(1)   a workbook on the topic 'Fire',
(2)   a video compilation of public information television features,
(3)   a slide presentation by a fire officer,
(4)   a video tape of the typical day of a fire fighter, and
(5)   a film presentation by a fire officer.

Each of the assignments involved a series of drafts. To enable pupils, teachers and researchers to appreciate the changes made at each draft, printouts were taken. Additionally, the researchers observed the children and recorded their discussions concerning their collaborative compositions which provided opportunities for a closer examination of the processes by which the written product was achieved. The word processor, as a research instrument, became the means of rendering composing and editing procedures susceptible to study.

Method and organisation

The collection of data was accomplished in a variety of ways during the research project. The researchers had chosen to work mainly within what might be called the illuminative paradigm of research using participant observation, recording the processes and interactions observed in diary form, backed up by tape transcripts and the printouts of all the drafts made by the children. The observation and teaching entailed the presence in school of one full-time researcher and one part-time researcher who made notes and compared observations as the programme developed. The presence of the one full-time researcher in the school over the period of a term also enabled notes to be taken on how the use of word processing facilities was being received by the staff and the other pupils in the school. Information on this aspect of the work was gained mainly through informal interviews and the spontaneous comments of staff and pupils.

Analysis

The analysis of the outcome presented here relates to such issues as the interaction of the pupils with each other and the word processing facilities; the organisation and sequencing of composing and drafting procedures; the editing outcomes: pupils' behaviour over a fairly broad area of the language arts.

Researchers noted that children were generally:

(1)   mutually supportive and co-operative in their collaborative groups,
(2)   unintimidated by the word processor system – microcomputer, monitor, disk drive and printer, and
(3)   inquisitive and innovative in their use of the word processor facilities.

The analysis of the observation notes, the transcripts of recorded children's discussions and the printouts of every draft of each assignment have yielded information on the children's strategies in word processing and their stages in producing text. This information has been examined in the context of current work on children's writing processes, particularly the work of Donald Graves.

In *Writing: Teachers and Children at Work* (Graves, 1982) it is pointed out that all children are conscious of encountering a sequence of obstacles in their development as writers. These are defined as:

(1)   spelling,
(2)   motor-aesthetic – concern over presentation and neatness,
(3)   convention – concern over 'orthodoxy' of punctuation and form,
(4)   information – concern over content, and
(5)   revision.

Kleiman and Humphrey (1982) note that children who compose on a word processor also follow a sequence of editing strategies concerned with:

(1)   the correction of errors in spelling, typing and punctuation,
(2)   the addition and substitution of words, clauses and sentences, and
(3)   the re-organisation of material.

Kane (1983) studying five eighth-grade students at the Bank Street School for Children composing individually on word processors, observed that production was primarily linear and sequential, and that most revisions were corrections in spelling and punctuation, though occasionally a single word or phrase was inserted or replaced.

The children studied in the project appeared at first to assimilate word processing to their conventional model of composing on paper by collaborating in the production of faultless text, painstakingly correcting errors perceived during composition by deleting and retyping. The corrections with which the children were observed to be concerned initially were those aspects of composition which Graves defines as 'spelling' and 'convention'. However, the children's increasing keyboard competence and their growing consciousness of the mutability of word processor text, contributed to a re-appraisal of their composing procedures. The correction of perceived errors was postponed until a draft neared completion and was achieved by more efficient facilities such as INSERT, OVER-WRITE and SEARCH AND REPLACE.

Kleiman and Humphrey (1982) note that, while writing 'requires both the mental processes of composing text and the physical aspects of producing it . . . word processing makes the physical aspects of producing and editing text much easier, so more attention can be devoted to the mental aspects'.

Observations indicate that children, relieved by a word processor of the 'motor-aesthetic' aspect of writing, are inclined to write more often and at greater length. Moreover, children who become familiar with the editing facilities of the word processor are aware of the mutable nature of their composition and are undaunted by the need for revision.

While the children involved in the N.E.L.P. research increased the length of their compositions at each draft, analysis of the relevant printouts revealed a tendency to progress from extension of the text by the addition of material toward expansion within the text by insertion (see Example 1). This phenomenon relates closely to the procedures which Graves has observed when studying children's customary (i.e. non-micro) drafting.

Example 1: The Deadly Fan Heater

Second Draft with *Extension* and *Revisions*.

Me and my sister were in bed at the time when the fire started. The plug on the fan heater blew up and started the fire.

We couldn't get out so we shouted for help. Our mum heard us and phoned the Fire Brigade.

It *takes* [1] the Fire Brigade eight minutes to get to *a fire*. [2] But in *six* [3] minutes the fire had got really violent. We threw our mattresses out, we were just about to jump when my sister said, 'Only jump as the last resort.' But we had to jump anyway.

Luckily we landed on the mattresses and got away with minor injuries. *The firemen were just rolling out the hoses and in no time at all the fire was out.*

A few days later we were out of hospital and moved into our new home. When we grew up I became a fireman and my sister is still trying to become a firewoman. [4]

[1] substitution for *took*
[2] substitution for *our house*
[3] substitution for *that eight*
[4] extension

Third Draft with *Revisions*.

Me and my sister were in bed at the time when the fire started. The plug on the fan heater *which was outside our door* [1] blew up *because it had been left on all night* [2] and started the fire. *So you could say that it was our fault.* [3]

We couldn't get out *because the fire was outside our door* [4] so we shouted for help. Our mum heard us and phoned the Fire Brigade.

It *took* [5] the Fire Brigade eight minutes to get to *our* [5] fire. But in *that eight* [7] minutes the fire had got really violent.

We took our quilts off our beds and put them against the gap under the door to stop the smoke getting into the room. [8] We *then opened the window and* [9] threw our mattresses out, we were just about to jump when my sister said, 'Only jump as a last resort.' But we had to jump anyway *because the fire was too near.* [10]

Luckily we landed on the mattresses and got away with minor injuries. The firemen were just rolling out the hoses *and some were jetting out water.* [11,12,13] In no time at all the fire was out.

A few days later we were out of hospital and moved into our new home. When we grew up I became a fireman and my sister is still trying to become a firewoman.

[1] insertion
[2] insertion
[3] insertion
[4] insertion
[5] substitution for *takes*
[6] substitution for *a*
[7] substitution for *six*
[8] insertion
[9] insertion
[10] insertion
[11] insertion
[12] omission of *and*
[13] creation of sentence

In addition, there were two aspects of the work which were useful in providing the children with the opportunity for exploring and making explicit to themselves concepts of story. These were:

(1) the accessibility of the text and ease of manipulation, and
(2) the group composing organisation and discussion that went on among the pupils.

While the story assignment (weeks two to four) – concerning a fire in the home, late at night – required the children to collaborate in composing, critically reading and revising their own work, the informational writing assignment (weeks seven to nine) required in addition that the children read a variety of source materials and incorporate the information gleaned into a leaflet directed at a different audience – younger children.

Analysis of the children's discussions while carrying out this task makes it quite clear that a wide range of reading skills was being employed:

(1) the recognition and selection of important detail,
(2) the re-organisation of items of information, and
(3) the evaluation of the usefulness of the information and its relevance and appeal to the envisaged audience.

In both of these writing assignments – the story and the informational leaflet – the nature of additional material, in both expansions and extensions, and the way in which entire compositions were subsequently re-organised, indicated the particular aspects of the writing task to which the children were beginning to pay attention. Notably, the children showed a developing grasp of appropriateness and effectiveness of text, the need for focus, and a sense of audience and of purpose (see Example 2).

Example 2: Fire Safety

Hi Kids,[1]
    I'm Freddy the Fire guard who protects you from fire. I'd like to talk to you about the fire that kills. If a fire started would you know what to do? I doubt it. So here's your chance to learn. I'm going to tell you [2]
some ways that fire
starts. One of the main
reasons is matches.
Children play with these
sometimes and can get
hurt very badly. If you see someone playing with these tell them not to it's dangerous.
    There are other causes of fire too. You're all probably playing on your electric games having fun but STOP. Look at the plug socket. If there are too many plugs in the socket it could easily

overheat and cause a terrible fire. So try not to overload them. When you finish whatever you are doing always switch off the plugs and take them out of the socket.

If people are careless with fire it can be very dangerous around the house. One of the golden fire rules is to shut all doors before going to bed. A door only holds fire back for 20 minutes and fire spreads FAST. This gives you time to get out SAFELY.

Your Mum can also make silly mistakes which [3] can cause fires. Some mums are very careless in the kitchen, they put too much fat in the chip pan and when she places the chips in the pan the fat overflows and can catch alight.

Smoking is another cause of fire. We all know that smoking is bad for our health but also if you do smoke stop and think. If your parents leave a cigarette end alight in an ashtray the cigarette would still be alight and could cause a ghastly fire.

If there is a mirror above a fire tell your mother to take it down because if someone gets too close their clothes could catch alight, they could get badly burnt. If your clothes do catch fire roll on the floor and don't panic.

So remember NEVER FOOL WITH FIRE.

[1] the children embedded a command to double-space the original print-out: the leaflet occupied both sides of an A4 sheet.
[2] the children altered the embedded command determining the line length to create this space for illustration.
[3] the children embedded a command for indentation to create this space for illustration.

One unexpected spin-off, in relation to the information storage and retrieval skills that the children were developing while becoming competent and confident users of disk and printout facilities, was that children on their own initiative, without any suggestion from the teachers or the researchers, began to make notes on aspects which they felt should be included in the informational leaflet prior to working on the word processor. It seems that composition and revision were not confined to the word processing sessions but had extended into their day to day classroom activities.

Conclusion

There are many areas of word processing in the primary school that remain to be explored. Results of the project so far have been very encouraging. There has been a very high level of enthusiasm shown by the pupils who remained motivated throughout. A study of the texts which were produced and of the processes which were involved has given us some confidence in saying that the word processor, considered as a resource for the development of children's writing, reading and comprehension, is well worth looking at in terms of the language arts, in both the primary and the secondary sector, with possible implications for the curriculum as a whole.

We have begun to look at children's approaches to word processing and their interactions while working at the facilities. We have drawn up tentative sequences in the operation of editing strategies and drafting procedures. We have looked at a variety of Pedagogic strategies for the use of word processors including individual, small group and, in our most recent work, large group use of the facilities. We have also made a start at looking in more depth at the language activities related to word processing – the language about language that takes place while the groups of children work.

The teachers involved in the project have subsequently introduced word processing as classroom practice – the school, having acquired during the project a second B.B.C. Model B, has fitted both of the microcomputers with 'Wordwise' and also acquired a disc drive and a printer. We have been able to introduce a larger number of teachers to the use of word processor facilities through in-service work, and with them we are continuing some of our investigations.

Acknowledgements

The authors wish to express their gratitude to the pupils, staff and the head-teacher of William Bellamy Junior School, Dagenham, in which the research was conducted.

References

GRAVES, D. (1982) *Writing: Teachers and Children at Work*. London: Heinemann.

KANE, J. (1983) 'Computers for Composing'. Paper presented at the Annual Meeting of the American Educational Research Association, April.

KLEIMAN, G. and HUMPHREY, M. (1982) 'Word Processing in the Classroom'. *Compute*, 22 (March).

OLDS, H. (1982) 'Word processing. How will it shape the student as a writer?' *Classroom Computer News*, November/December.

POTTER, F. (1984) 'Exploring the use of microcomputers in language and reading: breaking away from drills and programmed instruction', in D. Dennis (ed) *Reading: Meeting Children's Special Needs* (U.K.R.A. Proceedings, 1983) London: Heinemann.

ROWNTREE, D. (1974) *Educational Technology in Curriculum Development*. London: Harper and Row.

SAGE, M. and SMITH, D. J. (1983) *Microcomputers in Education: A Framework for Research*. London: S.S.R.C.

16   Write first, then read

James M. Wallace

> At the beach
> I found a pit.
> I playd in the pit.
> my mom and dad bout two and half pounds of
> salt water taffy.
> I wrote a note and roled it up and put it in a
> bottle I thre it in the ochen
> I flew a kite the kite flew off the string.

The author of this narrative is a curly-haired six-year-old boy who is in his last month of kindergarten. He printed the story on wide-lined pink primary paper and then propped it up on the back of the I.B.M. Selectric III so he could read it as he typed. When I sat down next to him on a low chair, knees tucked under my chin, he ignored me completely, but continued to type, searching the keyboard with intense concentration for each letter. When he finished, I asked 'Can you read me your story?' He did so, rapidly and accurately. Next question, 'Do you like to type?' 'Yes.' Final question, 'What do you like best in here?' 'The computer.'

In another school a kindergarten girl brings her printed story to a visiting administrator. The text reads, 'I see a hors and she is thinking about another hors.' The cartoon-style illustration shows a large horse with a thought-balloon over her head; inside the balloon is a smaller horse. The administrator says, 'I like it', and the girl runs cheerfully off to her next activity.

At a third school I find this story on the bulletin board. 'I went to marys house on tuesday we turnd over puzl pecis and we āt mufins.' Tacked up nearby is this message from a boy who has brought his emotions to his writing: 'if thees are my tois wy cant i thrō them out of the window. if this is my bruther y cant i punch him.'

This forceful writing and invented spelling is being created by kindergarten and other primary students in a 'Writing to Read' programme in Portland, Oregon. The Portland schools, which joined the programme in autumn 1983, are drawing on the experience of other schools and districts which have worked with the system since 1977. The programme was developed by John Henry Martin, a retired educator who believed that children would learn to communicate more effectively and rapidly if their early education stressed writing first, rather than reading. Working from this assumption, he gradually created materials and learning sequences to try out with classrooms of children. He also persuaded the International Business Machines Corporation (I.B.M.) to provide typewriters, personal computers, cassette players, and printed materials needed for experimentation with the system.

The Writing to Read system has received much attention in both the educational and the popular press. Its early results have been positive enough so that a number of writers have hailed it as a possible partial solution to America's literacy crisis. At the request of Martin and of I.B.M. the prestigious Educational Testing Service is conducting an extensive analysis of the system. And individual districts, such as Portland, are carrying on their own evaluations.

For those of us influenced by the educational ideas of John Dewey, Sylvia Ashton-Warner, Paolo Freire, and the language-experience approach, the system has a strong attraction. It begins with the natural language of children and provides a variety of ways for them to express that language. It proceeds from the assumption that children are curious about language, as about other aspects of their lives, and that, with support and encouragement, they will use that curiosity to develop their power over language. It begins with the active process of writing rather than the (usually) more passive process of reading. It stresses creation first, followed by correctness later. It uses student 'errors' (they are not so labelled) as a means of learning about the inconsistencies of English spelling. Although its developers do not so describe it, the system appears to put the old progressive wine of 'learning by doing' in the new bottles of advanced technology.

All this was intriguing enough to me so that I recently undertook my own search for usable truths about Writing to Read. This search led me to five of the fourteen schools in which Portland is trying out the system, to administrators who are responsible for implementing and monitoring it, and to researchers evaluating it. Consistent with the Writing to Read approach, in my description I will stress the process of this inquiry as much as the products of it.

I began by trying to get a child's-eye-view of the programme. I did this literally, attempting whenever possible to sit down next to students on little plastic chairs, seeing the equipment, materials, and adults from their perspectives. A typical class begins as a classroom of kindergarten children, accompanied by their teacher, comes into the Writing to Read (hereafter W.T.R.) laboratory. They look like they have been assembled for a United Nations Day presentation: blacks, whites, Asians, redheads, blondes, brunettes. There are 22 of them, and they fan out around the room going to their pre-assigned stations. Four sit down at the typewriters and begin to compose or to type stories they have printed by hand. Three pick up 'Punch-a-Shape' cards (not part of W.T.R.) and learn the shapes of letters by punching them out. Four go to stations where they follow along in picture books while they listen to taped stories. Three go to a writing table to compose their own stories on wide-lined paper. Four work at a table where they trace letters in work journals. And four go to computer terminals, put on earphones, and type words in response to printed, graphic, and auditory messages.

There are four adults helping them: their teacher, an aide, a building W.T.R. coordinator, and a parent volunteer. They move unobtrusively around the room helping students remember where they left off yesterday, suggesting starting points for today's activities, finding materials, and encouraging their efforts to learn.

The atmosphere is that of a good kindergarten room: students are interested but not frantic, there is a pleasant murmur of conversation, children work together at various learning centres, adults are quietly easing students into learning activities. The difference is in the technological richness of the room. In addition to the usual papers, pencils, chalk, workbooks, games, puzzles and books, there are tape players, I.B.M. Selectric III typewriters and I.B.M. personal computers. By late spring, most of the students seem to feel as comfortable with all this machinery as with the more traditional classroom materials. They insert paper into the typewriters, search out the letters they want, press the return key and space bars, and back-space when they want to make corrections. They find the tapes which match the books they want to read and insert them in the cassette players. They require more help with the computers, but work quite skilfully on particular sequences. The computer is seen as the new element of the programme, so let's watch a small curly-haired blonde girl as she works with the system. She sits down at the computer, a boy at her side, and puts on earphones. The teacher inserts the diskette for Cycle 3, and gets the program started. A picture of a leg appears on the screen along with the letters l-e-g. The picture disappears and the word remains. In response to audio instructions, the girl presses the letters l-e-g on the key-board. As she finishes this, the letters return to their proper places around the margin of the screen. The audio tells her again to write l-e-g and she again spells it out on the screen. The letters l-e-g shimmer and move on the screen, helping the girl to focus on them and to ignore any distractions (which are, in fact, minimal in this room). After satisfactorily completing this process she goes on to the word 'three'.

This girl has already learned, through the first two cycles, to write 'cat, dog, fish, pig, sun, and bed'. In cycle three she has learned 'rabbit', and is now practising with 'leg' and 'three'. As she completes the ten cycles she will learn to type 30 words. The computer will not insist on correct spelling, but will accept any phonetic spelling which accurately represents the sounds of the various words being taught. The girl and her fellow students learn, through these computer programs, how to use the 26 letters and the 42 phonemes they will need to write English phonetically.

A shift to the perspective of adults may help to put this girl's experience in context. As I visited classrooms, most aides, teachers, and parents were so busy helping children that I asked them few questions. I did observe, however, that they were calm, patient and helpful. The equipment and activities were so engrossing to most students that the adults could concentrate on the human parts of their work; motivating students, encouraging them, helping them get 'unstuck', prompting them to talk about what they had written or read. But between periods I was able to get some responses to the programme. One aide said that she likes W.T.R. because 'the kids *do* something – and think'. A parent volunteering with her son's class expressed enthusiasm for the programme's stress on phonics. She liked working with W.T.R. because it enabled her to give her son realistic help at home.

However, the greatest enthusiasm for W.T.R. was expressed by district curriculum administrators and the building co-ordinators of the programme.

One noted that students come to school wanting to write, and W.T.R. enables them to do so quickly and satisfyingly. He noted that, because the children are interacting with the computer, they feel that they are in partial control of what they learn. Another stressed the advantage that students have when they get early familiarity with the keyboard, both on the typewriter and on the computer. He also described W.T.R. as an excellent remedial programme for students who had difficulty with phonics. Another said that the programme is very motivating for students, that the learning stations help them focus on specific skills, and that W.T.R. is 'the best available application of the language-experience approach combined with technology'.

But school personnel are not being swept off their feet by the system. Most have been around schools long enough that they have seen various panaceas come and go. They are willing to give the programme a good try, but are not blind to its defects. They notice the occasional student sitting bored at the computer after too many repetitions of 'rabbit', and hit the 'escape' button for him or her. They see deficiencies in workbooks, such as the lack of directionality signs to help students form letters easily. They see the need for a better integration of writing and reading activities, and for some emphasis on comprehension. Several noted that students object to the unnuaturally slow pace of the reading on the tapes. Some noted that the programme still needs to develop more sophisticated and more interactive software. But all six of the administrators and co-ordinators with whom I talked see these as problems that can be gradually worked out, either by national W.T.R. developers or by district personnel. All see the programme as helpful to children and want to continue to work with it.

With these mostly positive impressions in mind, I next went to the Portland schools' new administration building, where I had been invited to sit in on a meeting of researchers who are responsible for monitoring and evaluating the system. One of them described their three-year task of evaluating an over-publicised programme: in the first year they will 'just blow the foam off it'; the second will be a 'shake-down' year; and the third will be the real evaluation year.

Their effort will supplement the Educational Testing Service (E.T.S.) study of W.T.R. Only 15 of Portland's classrooms are included in the E.T.S. sample, but Portland will study all 64 of the district's participating classes (approximately two-thirds kindergarten, one-third first grade, and a few second grades). E.T.S. is not doing systematic observations, but Portland will conduct three one-hour observations in each of 26 W.T.R. laboratories. The California Test of Basic Skills will be used to evaluate progress in W.T.R. classrooms and in control-group classrooms. This only begins to suggest the complexity of the task facing Portland's researchers. Holding all variables constant is as challenging as getting a roomful of squirming first-graders to sit still on Friday afternoon. Some of the students have had pre-kindergarten and some have not, some are in half-day kindergartens and others attend all day. Little baseline data is available and different schools provide varied amounts of staff support.

In the light of these difficulties, the main message from the evaluators was:

interpret your impressions cautiously. They are still smarting from the response to a recent report in which the Portland Research and Evaluation Department said, 'Our existing efforts to use Computer-Assisted Instruction in the elementary schools are overall a failure.' This was not the message that some administrators had expected and wanted to hear. And, in the light of strong administrative support for W.T.R. the researchers want a very careful evaluation of the system. They already anticipate that their interpretations of it may not be as 'upbeat' as those which will come out of the Educational Testing Service. As one of them said, 'It is likely that the national results will be positive or construed as positive.' He warned against a 'market-driven bias' in the E.T.S. evaluation. And, in the light of broad claims for W.T.R. effects, he noted that it may be only a way of 'accelerating movement through a narrow range of skills'.

In spite of their research-oriented caution, the evaluators were willing to speculate briefly about future possibilities for W.T.R. One noted that W.T.R. may provide a means of encouraging teachers to use a language-experience approach to teaching reading and writing. Another suggested that it might work most effectively as part of a true continuous progress model. But they left big questions in my mind. Given the expense of W.T.R. in personnel, time, hardware and materials, could equal or better results be obtained through other means? If the system turns out to be as effective as claimed, is this a result of the teaching strategy, the particular equipment and programs, or some combination of the two?

So my search for a usable truth about Writing to Read goes on. And I continue it with the enthusiasm of the participants and the caution of the evaluators. I will be eager to see if the participants can sustain their initial optimism as they and the evaluators try to sort out what is really at work here: new technology? more sophisticated learning sequences? new teacher roles? learning stations? student choice and motivation? The word 'motivation' suggests one of the keys, and brings us back to the father of progressive education, John Dewey. As I sat in different classrooms, watching six-year-olds manipulate the latest products of the industrial age, I wondered what Dewey would make of all this. As I saw children working with computers, typewriters, teachers and each other, I recalled Dewey's persuasive words:

> Methods for learning to read come and go across the educational arena like the march of supernumeraries upon the stage. Each is heralded as the final solution of the problem of learning to read; but each, in turn, gives way to some later discovery. The simple fact is, that they all lack the essential of any well-grounded method, namely relevance to the child's mental needs. No scheme for learning can supply this want.
>
> Only a new motive – putting the child in a vital relation to the things to be read – can be of service here.

The Writing to Read system assumes that students will have the most 'vital relation' with their own thoughts and words and those of their fellow learners. And it provides a means by which children can quickly and creatively learn to express their ideas through invented spelling which makes sense to them. With a realistic understanding of the phonetic basis of English writing, they can then securely and confidently deal with the complexities and inconsistencies of 'book spelling'.

If Writing to Read, and comparable systems, fulfil their early promise, teachers will have to continue and intensify the challenge of redefining their roles. They will spend less time in transmitting information and conducting drills, and more in helping students assess their 'mental needs' and develop 'vital relations' with the real and symbolic worlds. They need not fear being replaced by technology as they find their instructional skills enhanced by it.

Students are also struggling with these complicated relationships between themselves, the new technologies, and their teachers. Given the objectives of the Writing to Read system, it is appropriate to give the last word on this subject to one of Portland's six-year-old authors. As she tries to figure out what she likes best in the Writing to Read laboratory, she finally decides it is the teacher to whom she addressed this message,

I liket the tipe riter Best of all
and I like to work with you.
And I liket lisoning to the story's
But best I like working with you.

References

DEWEY, J. (1972), originally published (1898) 'The Primary-education fetich'. *John Dewey: The Early Works*, Vol.5. Carbondale: Southern Illinois University Press, pp.259–64.
HAWKINS, P. (1982) 'A test of the theory that children could learn to read by first learning to write'. *IPD News*, I (3). White Plains, N.Y.: International Business Machines, pp.1–7.
ETS to evaluate 'Writing to Read' (1983) *ETS Developments* (Summer).
'Evaluation report on computer use in the Portland public schools' (1983). Portland, Oreg.: Research and Evaluation Department, Portland Public Schools, p.70.
LEONARD, G. (1984) 'The great school report hoax'. *Esquire*, pp.47–56.
'On Reading, writing, and computers: a conversation with John Henry Martin' (1981). *Educational Leadership* (October), pp.60–64.

17 Microcomputer generated speech and C.A.L. programs for remedial reading

R. J. Eyre and C. D. Terrell

Until recently designers of computer-assisted learning (C.A.L.) programs have had to assume that the learner will be able to use a conventional QWERTY keyboard and read information presented on a printer/screen. Because of this C.A.L. programs have remained unavailable to many of those who might most benefit from it, e.g., young children and those older children and adults who have learning problems. The development of inexpensive speech generation systems now allows computers to 'talk' to those who cannot read and facilitate the production of effective C.A.L. programs to meet the needs of those with learning difficulties.

Methods of speech generation

There are two primary methods of microcomputer speech generation: construction synthesis and analysis synthesis (Frantz, Schalk and Woodson, 1982).

Construction synthesis

Speech is generated from a library of prefabricated speech tokens. Spoken English can be broken down into about 42 phonemes and, using an appropriate set of rules, these can be strung together to form comprehensible speech. Systems using this technique (theoretically) provide the user with an unlimited vocabulary. In practice, however, about 5 per cent of words are unintelligible but this can be overcome by selecting the vocabulary to suit the phonemic tokens and rules. The major disadvantage, for educational applications, is that the speech has a pronounced robotic quality. Terrell and Linyard (1982) report that, although children find a robotic voice intelligible and acceptable, remedial reading teachers find it unacceptable.

Analysis synthesis

Speech generated by this method has a human quality because individual words are pre-recorded by a human speaker and stored on a chip. The quality of reproduction is such that the speech characteristics (accent, etc.) of the original speaker can be identified and teachers find this speech acceptable. The major disadvantage is that it can only be used in applications which require a limited vocabulary because it is expensive in terms of computer storage. Developments in techniques of data compression and increases in memory availability are rapidly decreasing these problems (Kourra, 1982).

The programs

The C.A.L. programs described here were developed to assist with remedial reading. Initially two types of demonstration program were written: one used constructive synthesis and the other analysis synthesis. These were shown to teachers on in-service courses who overwhelmingly favoured the programs using analysis synthesis and, therefore, this method of speech generation was used in all subsequent programs.

There are a variety of ways of teaching early reading skills but, no matter which method is preferred by a particular school, clinic or teacher, at some stage the learner reads a text whilst an 'expert reader' provides some form of prompt when the learner is 'stuck'. This is very expensive in terms of resources because it is one-to-one teaching at its most intensive. It is, however, quite a simple and repetitive task which could be handled by a micro-computer. The programs described here take over this aspect of reading instruction in an effective and interesting way.

When one of the programs is run the first page of a beginning reader appears on the screen complete with picture and text. A line appears under the first word of the text and the reader can advance this line along the text by pressing one of the microcomputer keys. Every time the key is pressed the line moves to the next word (just like reading by pointing with the finger). The child reads at his or her own pace, while moving the line under the text. Whenever the child comes to a word he or she cannot read, simply pressing the space bar will cause the microcomputer to 'say' that word, i.e., whichever word is currently underlined will be spoken when the space bar is depressed. The microcomputer has a friendly female voice. The space bar and two keys (one to advance the line and one to move it backwards) are the only controls the learner needs to use.

The program's graphics are all in full colour. Pictures on the screen are always related to the text, giving the child essential clues as to the meaning of the text. The programs use a limited vocabulary suitable for beginning readers and are intended for use in the home or school. It is recommended that they be used in the following way. The child is given a book to read in the form of a C.A.L. program. Each book is on a disk or cassette. To operate the programs neither teacher nor child need have any computer knowledge. The child works through each (C.A.L.) book at his/her own pace, asking for prompts from the computer whenever required. When feeling confident of knowing all the words in the book, the child returns to the teacher and demonstrates his or her skill by reading to the teacher. The teacher will always have the text of the book that appeared on the screen printed in the form of a conventional book. The programs are not intended as a substitute for the teacher. They are primarily aimed at making small group teaching more effective by providing a one-to-one teaching situation whilst at the same time freeing the teacher to deal with other children in the group.

The programs keep a record of what the child is doing whilst working alone at the microcomputer. Each word the child asks for help with can be listed on a screen/printer at the end of each session. This is a very useful diagnostic aid and is a facility that has impressed many teachers because the learners' activities are being monitored for the entire time they are using the programs.

Discussion

This mode of learning is particularly suitable for children with specific reading difficulties. These children often feel very uncomfortable and anxious during reading instruction because, no matter how sympathetic the teacher, the pupil is always conscious of making mistakes, in the presence of another person, on a task which is apparently very simple for everybody else. These C.A.L. programs appear to reduce these difficulties because they are infinitely patient and intrinsically unthreatening to these children. Preliminary trials indicate that children with special needs enjoy using this type of C.A.L. program.

References

FRANTZ, G. A., SCHALK, T. B. and WOODSON, L. (1982) 'Voice synthesis and recognition'. *Mini-Micro Systems* (December), pp.146–60.

KOURRA, L. (1982) 'Speaking machines – an engineering reality'. *Engineering Materials and Design* (January), pp.11–17.

TERRELL, C. D. and LINYARD, O. (1982) 'The evaluation of electronic learning aids: The Texas Instruments Speak Spell', *The International Journal of Man Machine Studies*, 17(1), pp.59–67.

18 Storytelling and beginning reading: the use of a microcomputer to facilitate storytelling by nursery school children

Helen C. Tite

Accepting a computer as a direct substitute for the first-hand experience of books limits the potential of the young child's investigation and self discovery about the communication process, both oral and written. In using a computer and adopting an exploratory approach I hope to indicate some of the potential a computer offers to the teacher of language and reading in early education.

Software for the development of language and reading available to teachers tends to emphasise skill acquisition. There is also a need for young children to be able to comprehend and build understandings about the process of reading so that they can develop their own strategies to acquire the technique of reading. Teachers need to have insights into how children comprehend the reading process. A microcomputer was used in a controlled experiment to evaluate the use of a computer program in its effort to elicit a story form from young children (Tite, 1983).

In drawing forth a story form it was hoped that the insights gained would offer an approach to beginning reading based on children's understanding of text as a set of connected ideas.

Comprehension of story as a structure

Research literature offers evidence to suggest that the understanding children have of story as a structured form is a developmental one (Applebee, 1978). In his analysis of stories by children from 2 to 17 years of age, Applebee identified stages of development in the formation of a concept of story. The insights provided suggest that the stories children compose show their mastery of literary form. Coupland (1982) suggests that readers have a natural ability to summarise a plot whilst ignoring unnecessary detail. Coupland explored the structural analysis of narratives to highlight unseen textual characteristics which may affect reader response, identifying the narrative structure as a complete, linear, sequential, structural analysis of text. She found that when the structural sequence of narrative units was altered, the reader's comprehension was affected. It would appear therefore that story structure supports comprehension by providing a framework for the plot, erasing detail which may distract the reader and thereby aids comprehension. In any subsequent reading or re-telling of a story, the structure offers a framework of expectations about plot development and so aids comprehension.

Is the ability to perceive structure a fundamental skill required for beginning reading and developing strategies to acquire reading technique?

Would young children's storytelling and experience with books provide them with the understandings that text is a set of connected ideas and that the author creates a text? Bower (1976) provided evidence of how adults process and understand text. The following insights can be drawn from his study:

simple stories/folk tales have a definite structure;
from experiencing stories people acquire an abstract framework;
if a text violates a critical rule of structure then the text seems less coherent; and
the structure of a story may be distinguished from its content.

There is a lack of empirical evidence to support the premise that an understanding of story as a structure is tied in to beginning reading, but the question is raised as to whether any child begins to read without having first established a sound concept of story. The implication for the teacher in promoting language and reading development is that time should be taken to observe children's behaviours, identifying those children who do not seem to pay attention to books or make little attempt to find meaning in their experiences with books and stories in their play.

The computer program

A computer program was designed to provide a picture story in high resolution graphics. The story was an original one, constructed to match the age interests of 3- to 5-year-old children, in content and form. This was then interpreted as a collection of images and computed to produce a static picture on the screen. A story structure is simulated by changing one of the elements of the picture at a time such as moving the position of a bird in the sky to a position on the grass at the press of a key. The sequence becomes apparent as the key is operated to make changes within the picture. Each child viewed the sequence of modifications to the picture on the screen and then began their story with the prompt 'Once upon a time'. The changes were made on screen as the child responded with a narrative.

For some children their narrative consisted of identifying the elements of the picture on the screen, while for other children the changes on the screen were utilised in their narratives to produce a story with simple structure. The stories began by setting the scene and involved the two characters in a set of related ideas ending with a simple climax. It could be speculated that those children who were able to produce such stories offered evidence of their perception of story structure derived from hearing stories told or read to them.

An orientation to literacy?

How is the child started in this orientation to books and stories? Clark (1976) found that the common experiences of young fluent readers provided insights. Since then there has been a growing number of studies of young children and their experiences with books and storytelling. The most dramatic of these is the record by Butler (1979) who presents the developing awareness of stories and books of a very young child, Cushla, who was physically disabled and intellectually handicapped. Cushla's understanding of books and stories began when she was nursed as an infant by both parents in turn to keep her interested and occupied to overcome the distress of her disabilities. As she grew older, fragments of story were held onto by the child, those which provided emotional satisfaction through the text and a sensory response to the colours and shapes in the illustrations. Cushla adopted phrases and sentences from favourite stories which were read and re-read on demand by her parents. These were transferred to her everyday experience as appropriate to her.

'Let's walk home it's time for tea' (from *Mr Gumpy's Outing*, by John Burningham). This was used to terminate a family visit to the beach when Cushla wanted to go home for her tea. Her everyday interaction with a wide range of children's literature, from which she could select and which she could have repeatedly read to her by a responsive adult, is an indication of the effect of storytelling experiences in orientating a young child to the text in books and in promoting language expression. At six years of age Cushla was reported to be reading fluently and this was without the aid of reading instruction.

Other studies highlight the use that very young children make of the stories in books, responding to illustrations and endeavouring to make sense of the reading behaviour of their parents (Bissex, 1980; Payton, 1984). A cross-cultural insight is offered by Scollon and Scollon (1981), who provide the observation of their two-year-old daughter Rachel being taught to read by a 10-year-old Athabaskan child in North America. The Athabaskan cultural expectations for oral story-making were superimposed on the written text in the following manner and provide a contrast between the two cultures in the response of the younger children.

The older sister attempted to teach her younger sister to read with a picture book first. The younger sister was five years old and was orientated to the social expectation of helping in the telling of stories by repeating lines by the Storyteller.

OS : because
YS : because
OS : a
YS : a
OS : giraffe
YS : giraffe
OS : might
YS : might
OS : look
YS : look
OS : sort of
YS : sort of
OS : silly
YS : silly

A short while later the older child sat with Rachel Scollon and repeated the activity saying she was going to teach Rachel to read as she had her own sister. She began in the same way as above but Rachel did not echo her response and anticipated it:

OS : because
R : because a goat might eat it for supper
OS : The whole thing!

After her surprise the older child again instructed Rachel to respond in the echoed response of the oral storytelling of the Athabaskan people. Rachel acquiesced. (p.60)

The Scollons put forward the argument that the form of literacy reflected in an oral tradition is an interactive one and the storytelling using books underlines the role of the parent or adult as mediator between the author and the text. The early experiences of the young child orientate the child to the literacy of the culture which has nurtured it. They saw their young daughter's behaviour as reflecting her experience of books and stories shared with them and the behaviour of the Athabaskan girls as reflecting the appropriate storytelling behaviour of the oral tradition of Fort Chipewaya. Other records of insights into the way in which the young children of a cultural group adopt the behaviours of the adults are Munn (1963) and Reeves (1964), who provide such evidence of Australian aboriginal children responding to the legends and storytelling tradition of their tribes and adopting the appropriate behaviours. An American survey by Cappa (1958) identifies kindergarten children's desire to have stories repeated which have already been read to them. Such a desire suggests an attempt to understand stories and books.

Building an understanding of text

A study by Lomax (1979) focused on nursery children's awareness and appreciation of the written word through their response to books and stories. She concluded that a child may ignore an activity at school because of the lack of such experience in the home, that is with books and stories. Repeated experiences with stories and books may offer to children the opportunity they want to make sense of stories as language behaviour. The behaviour of a reader who seems able to bring to life and reconstruct stories in the same sequence as the pictures in a book but also with the same formal sentence structure when the story is re-read provides a model to imitate, so that behaviours are copied and an effort is made to understand what is happening. Wade (1983) identifies the reader-like behaviour of Rowena who plays out the adult role of reading a story book. Wade's analysis of Rowena's narrative suggests that her storytelling has shape and meaning with intonation contributing strongly to the notion of a story.

Observations of two four-year-olds in nursery school wearing radio mikes offered this simulated reading of a picture book. Two Mr Men books were selected from the books available. The 'Mr Mean' storybook was used to begin and then changed in favour of 'Mr Messy', although Mr Mean is the central character. The child imitated the reading behaviour and expressive language of books as she had assimilated them. Her peer, who could read, held a doll which she used to try and take over the role of reader. An adult briefly supported the play situation.

A : You're her big sister are you?
P : Yes.
C : Yes and I'm reading a story to her.
One day Mr Mean went out. He didn't know what to do so he went back in. (Mr Mean book replaced with Mr Messy.)
P : Let her have a read (the doll being held by P)
C : Just pretend she can talk and act naturally.
P : I'll hold her up.
C : And so . . . he didn't know what to do _____ [simulated words] but he didn't know what to do either. He shouted and shouted to Mr Messy. He opened every door and every . . . and every door and every window and every window and every . . . house! A purple house and a purple door and a yellow door and a red door. He didn't know what to do so he had a bath instead. Dolly stop it. Listen to the story!

The book was replaced with another one.

Is there a story structure of a beginning, a related set of ideas and an ending contained within her 'reading' of the two books? The pages were flipped over as she constructed her story for her pretend big sister with the doll on her lap. The pattern used by the child suggested that she was constructing a story while adopting the reading behaviour of holding a book and turning the pages in a left to right direction. As Wade suggests (1983), there was a strong sense of 'storying', that is, making a story with intonation contributing strongly to her 'reading'. She derived detail from the illustrations in both books but appeared non-plussed by the lack of support she got from them as she tried to interpret them. To identify it further in Bower's terms, it had a simple setting, characters and a problem to resolve (1976). Bower sees such a structure being used by adults to interpret texts as well as a guide to the construction of their own narratives of real life episodes.

The ability to construct their own composition may also help children's understanding of what it is to be an author and increase the likelihood that they would be able to anticipate the writing of another writer. Sulzby and Otto (1982) found that children who were higher in emergent reading abilities offered more clearly distinguishable texts and were able to talk about them.

The young child who has had experience of stories and books and developed an understanding of what constitutes a story may be enabled to find a matching story structure in the text, even to search for it. The experiences which we offer to young children should take account of the evidence which is being accumulated from research into narrative structure. The observation of children's early 'reading' behaviour may provide insights into their

141

developing understanding of story structure and their orientation to the text in books.

The orientation for some children to become literate appears to be part of a natural process. Why are some children missing out? Is their story experience meagre and not able to support learning to read? My own results in using a computer to facilitate storytelling suggest that while all the nursery school children could identify the notion of what a story is and attempt to tell one, there were those children whose concept of story was very primitive while other children appeared to have a sound concept of story and were able to structure a simple plot. This leads me to conclude that the opportunities offered to children may be only superficial, and teachers with the responsibility for language development should be far more aware of the children's ability to respond to stories and to tell their own stories.

The computer program designed to investigate young children's ability to structure a story offers a tool to teachers to identify those children who cannot structure a story, and who may be lacking in experience of hearing stories read and of browsing through books.

This suggests future approaches to support children in their orientation to become literate:

(1) Selection of stories to be based on children's observed play interests.
(2) Opportunities for children to request favourite stories to be repeated.
(3) Time to browse through books especially ones which have been read in group situations.
(4) Time given to reading stories to individual children with expectations for ancillary staff clearly defined to support children's interests in book selection.
(5) Books changed regularly so that children can find new books to suit their interests as well as the current favourites.
(6) Books on display to include nursery rhyme collections with clearly defined illustrations which support the text.
(7) Follow up opportunities for children to express story ideas in play with appropriate materials/props available.
(8) Selection of books to be based on criteria to meet the developmental story interests of the children.
(9) Make opportunities for children to tell their own stories.
(10) Type children's stories and collate into book with their drawings.
(11) Record children's spontaneous stories on audio tapes to play back to them.
(12) Provide storytelling packs of book and audio cassettes for children to listen to own choice of story when they wish to do so.

References

APPLEBEE, A. N. (1978) *The Child's Concept of Story*. London and Chicago: University of Chicago Press.

BISSEX, G. L. (1980) *GNYS AT WRK: A Child Learns to Write and Read*. Cambridge, Mass.: Harvard University Press.

BOWER, G. H. (1976) 'Experiments on story understanding and recall'. *Quarterly Journal of Experimental Psychology*, 28, pp.511–34.

BUTLER, D. (1979) *Cushla and Her Books*. London: Hodder & Stoughton.

CAPPA, D. (1958) 'Kindergarten children's spontaneous responses to storybooks read by teachers'. *Journal of Educational Research*, 52(2), p.75.

CAZDEN, C. B. (1976) 'Play with language and meta-linguistic awareness', in J. S. Bruner *et al.*, *Play: Its Role in Development and Evolution*. Harmondsworth: Penguin.

CLARK, M. M. (1976) *Young Fluent Readers. What Can they Teach us?* London: Heinemann Educational.

COUPLAND, J. (1982) 'What's in a story?: narrative structure and realisation in children's fiction', in Peter Hunt (ed) *Further Approaches to Research in Children's Literature*. Cardiff: University of Wales.

LOMAX, C. M. (1979) 'Interest in books and stories', in M. Clark and W. M. Cheyne, *Studies in Pre-School Education*. London: Hodder & Stoughton.

MUNN, M. D. (1963) 'The Walbiri sand story'. *Australian Territories*, 3(6), pp.37–44.

PAYTON, S. (1984) *Developing Awareness of Print. A Young Child's First Steps towards Literacy*. Educational Review Off-set Publication number 2, University of Birmingham.

REEVES, W. (1984) *The Legends of Moonie Jarl*. Queensland: The Jacaranda Press.

SCOLLON, R. and SCOLLON, S. (1981) *Narrative, Literacy and Face in Inter-Ethnic Communication*. New Jersey: Ablex.

SHAW, M. L. G. (1980) *On Becoming a Personal Scientist*. London: The Academic Press.

SPRAGUE MITCHELL, L. (1948) *The Here and Now Storybook*. (New York: E. P. Dutton.

SULZBY, E. and OTTO, B. (1982) '"Text" as an object of meta-linguistic knowledge: a study in literacy development'. *First Language*, 3, pp.181–99.

TITE, H. C. (1983) 'Storytelling and its link with beginning reading: an experiment in the use of computer graphics to elicit structure in storytelling'. Unpublished M.Ed. dissertation, University of Birmingham.

WADE, B. (1983) 'Story and intonation features in young children: a case study'. *Educational Review*, Special Issue (15), 35(2), pp.175–86.

19   Computer use in remedial reading programmes

Helen Mulholland

The remedial programmes described in this paper were designed on the basis of research findings regarding the nature of the interaction with text of failing and normal readers (Mulholland, 1984). By analysing responses to a cloze type of test, it was found that readers of different ages and levels of reading ability produced significantly different patterns of response. Mean scores rose with age and patterns of response changed between age 9 and age 12. After age 12, pupils of equivalent levels of reading ability produced the same types of responses with the same frequency.

The study

Six groups of teachers have been studied.

(1)   Twelve-year-olds with reading ages of approximately 12 years, as measured by the Schonell Silent Reading Test (Oliver & Boyd, 1971), are referred to as 'normal 12-year-olds'.

(2)   Twelve-year-olds with reading ages at least two years below their chronological ages, mean reading age approximately 9 years, are referred to as 'failing readers'.

(3)   Nine-year-olds with reading ages equivalent to their chronological ages are referred to as '9-year-olds'.

(4)   A sample drawn from the top 15 per cent of each year group in a secondary school, measured on the basis of cloze scores, is referred to as 'good readers'. Ages of this group are between 12 and 15.

(5)   Average readers in the same age range selected from the middle 15 per cent as measured by cloze scores.

(6)   Poor readers in the same age range come from the bottom 15 per cent.

Groups 4, 5 and 6 were created by amalgamating three separate age groups when it was found that for good and average readers there was no change in the pattern of response between the ages of 12 and 15. The only significant change in the responses of poor readers was an increasing ability to deal with whole sentences.

The responses of these groups of readers were classified by a system which relates responses to the type of information used, or mis-used, in their crea-

144

tion. While it is a subjective system, it has been used in the classification of over 200,000 responses and has not yet proved unworkable. More important, the results of the classification appear to contain some valuable information regarding the reading of the different groups of readers.

Classification of cloze responses

1. Verbatim (V): The exact word deleted.
2. Semantically-acceptable (SEMAC): A close synonym of the word deleted.
3. Zero (Z): No entry in a gap.

Group T: responses related to the theme of the text

4. TS: Errors of scanning:

caused by mis-reading or overlooking visual information.
e.g. He *fixed* at the tyre
(looked)

5. TC: Errors of chunking:

caused by wrong re-construction of local syntax.
e.g. His motor-bike was fast and loud and *just* like a plane taking off.
(sounded)

6. TV: Errors of vocabulary:

almost correct restoration of the original meaning, usually generalisations.
e.g. He was going up a high *slope*
(hill)

7. TE: Errors of expectation:

provides a text which is correct but differs in meaning from the original.
e.g. His long yellow *scarf* trailed out behind him.   (hair)

8. TH: Errors of hesitation:

caused by failing to read the following context.
e.g. His front tyre went flat with a *nail* like a gun.   (sound)

9. TR: Random errors:

words related to the theme of the text but with no apparent connection to the local context.
e.g. His long yellow *motor* trailed out behind him.   (hair)

Group N: responses not related to the theme of the text

10. NC: Correct within the
     sentence.   e.g. His long yellow *tail* trailed out
                                  behind him.   (hair)

11. NH: Correct according to
     the preceding part of
     the sentence but not the
     following part.   e.g. Alan Harper took the *dog* without
                                  slowing down.   (bend)

12. NP: Correct within the
     phrase, collocation.   e.g. His long yellow *daffodil* trailed out
                                  behind him.   (hair)

13. NN: Nonsense: no connection with any part of the
                                  text.

In giving results of the classification, frequencies of occurrence of each category have been converted to percentages of either Group T, those responses which relate to the theme of the text, or group N, responses produced by groups of readers when they are acknowledging the constraint of the theme and when they have abandoned it; this appears to represent a clear division in the pattern of responses. Since failing and poor readers are more likely to lose the theme, the conversion to these two separate percentages is necessary if valid comparisons are to be made (see Table 1).

Table 1: Patterns of response produced by different
groups of readers on cloze tests

Group of readers	Number of responses				Percentage of group in category							
	Group T	Group N	TS	TC	TV	TE	TH	TR	NC	NH	NP	NN
Normal 12	548	252	3	2	48	32	9	5	74	10	8	9
Nines	1060	473	3	5	38	27	14	12	53	21	9	17
Failing	912	626	7	3	41	23	19	8	49	17	9	25
Good	1002	166	3	3	32	51	10	0	36	11	46	7
Average	1450	431	3	4	29	48	14	2	34	17	35	14
Poor	1676	933	7	4	26	42	17	5	30	19	24	27

The characteristics of failing and poor readers which appear to distinguish them from other groups are:

(1) the tendency to ignore the theme of the text more frequently: large number of group N errors;

146

(2) increased incidence of errors of visual scanning, category TS;
(3) increased incidence of errors arising from lack of use of following context, categories TH and NH;
(4) less successful reconstruction of whole sentences when the theme of the text is ignored, category NC;
(5) higher incidence of nonsense responses bearing no relation to any part of the text, category NN.

Nine-year-olds appear to have more difficulties with syntax, category TC, and with using local context, category TR. They also tended to leave a larger number of items unanswered.

By looking at the responses of individual readers, it was possible to recognise areas in which remedial help appeared to be necessary. This help was given over a period of six months during one 40-minute period per week. Subjects were tested on the Schonell test at the beginning and the end of the programme and again one year later; no remedial help was given in the intervening year (see Table 2, page 148).

Since the results appear to be considerable, the exercises used in each area may be of interest. It is in this connection that the use of computer programs is discussed.

Exercises for visual scanning

The timed display facility of the microcomputer has been used in a variety of 'drill and practice' reading programs. Unfortunately these do not always involve the reader in any meaningful interaction with the text. Choosing a target word from a list was one low level exercise presented in several programs. Similar exercises on paper (Leslie and Calfee, 1971) have indicated that poor readers are not necessarily worse than good readers at this type of task and there would seem little to be gained from computer presentation. Grant and Peters (1981) suggest that visual processing difficulties arise from failure to control focusing along lines of print. A computer program was used which displayed a text as a series of phrases in rapid sequence, with each phrase appearing at its correct position on the screen. The reader had to follow visually the appearance of the text on the screen, comprehend the text and answer questions. Speed could be varied. The program utilised a 'whole reading' task but emphasised the visual scanning of print. It had the added advantage of separating text into phrases, which might help to develop recognition of phrase structure.

Table 2 shows that in the year in which no remedial help was given, errors of this type disappeared. This may suggest that practice in normal reading in the curriculum will itself overcome difficulties of this type where these are not severe. It seems that there is a need to consider not only the theoretical validity of drill and practice programs but also their comparative effectiveness.

Exercises to improve re-construction of syntax

Several programs ask the reader to re-arrange words, phrases or clauses to

Table 2: Diagnostic profiles of individual readers

Subject number	R.A. on Schonell R3 test	Number of responses of category													Total in group N
		V	S	Z	TS	TC	TV	TE	TH	TR	NC	NH	NP	NN	
1 a	8y7	11	9	0	3	2	6	4	6	0	9	2	4	4	19
b	11y4	22	11	0	1	0	5	7	5	1	3	2	3	0	8
c	13 +	28	9	0	0	2	5	8	1	1	2	3	1	0	6
2 a	8y2	11	11	1	3	2	4	2	5	5	4	5	4	3	16
b	10y5	19	8	1	2	0	3	7	4	2	3	1	7	3	14
c	13 +	9	6	21	0	0	4	6	3	1	5	1	3	1	10
3 a	7y6	13	5	0	3	0	7	3	8	4	3	6	2	6	17
b	12 +	25	4	1	1	0	7	5	4	2	3	2	5	2	12
c	13 +	24	10	1	0	0	8	5	2	0	4	2	3	1	10
4 a	8y7	14	8	0	2	0	6	9	6	0	7	3	2	3	15
b	10y5	21	11	0	3	0	5	6	5	0	4	1	2	2	9
c	13 +	27	11	0	0	1	3	7	3	0	2	0	3	3	8
5 a	8y11	16	10	5	2	0	3	7	4	2	3	3	3	2	11
b	11y4	25	11	1	0	0	3	7	3	2	2	2	2	2	8
c	13 +	26	10	11	0	1	1	4	2	0	3	0	1	1	5
6 a	8y7	17	6	1	3	0	4	5	4	3	5	3	4	5	17
b	10y3	35	7	0	1	0	5	8	6	1	0	2	4	1	7
c	10y3	33	6	0	0	1	6	9	3	0	1	0	1	0	2

a = pre-test results
b = results six months later, after remedial programme
c = results one year after b, with no further remedial help

V = exact word deleted
S = acceptable word
Z = no response

148

form sentences. Others ask for a given work to be fitted in at an appropriate point in a sentence. It would appear that such exercises are not required by the failing readers in secondary schools who do not make errors of syntax more frequently than normal readers. A third criterion for selection of computer programs in reading is therefore their applicability to the readers involved. The temptation to assume that use of a computer program in any area will strengthen performance in that area must be resisted in favour of a rigorous matching of programs to the needs of individual readers.

Exercises to improve vocabulary

Failing readers tended to use a more restricted lexicon than other groups in responding to cloze tests. 75 per cent of their errors were words which appear on the Dale–Chall list of 769 words likely to be known by eight-year-olds. Possible causes for the use of a restricted lexicon are the size of the lexicon, the efficiency of searching, the amount of attention available and the decision as to choice when words have been located. Biemiller (1970) found that 90 per cent of the substitution errors of beginning readers were words which they had encountered elsewhere in their reading; a similar effect may operate on failing readers whose reading materials have been restricted. In the absence of visual cues, they may prefer to choose words which they have encountered elsewhere in their reading.

To extend vocabulary, all exercises except those for visual scanning were made the focus for group discussion. Computer programs dealing with synonyms, antonyms and dictionary work provide a specific 'vocabulary' focus but do not generally require the use or application of the vocabulary except in sentence completion tasks. The restricted number of words dealt with in one run of the program generally causes a degree of over-simplification in these tasks.

Computer programs should provide an opportunity to use the reading or language skills in a more extended task.

Exercises to encourage the generation of alternative expectations

Constructivist views of the reading process would regard the generation of errors of expectation, category TE, as a 'good' reading behaviour. Failing readers require to be encouraged in this practice. Prediction exercises in which the reader is given one segment of a text and asked to predict what will be the following part have been well established as paper excercises. Their translation to computer programs is made difficult by the open-ended type of response which is required. All suggestions must be accepted and tested against the cues in the text; there can be no finite pre-existing data base.

In choosing computer programs, it is necessary to consider whether the use of the computer is as effective as ordinary paper exercises or whether the extra time involved in creating the computer program is justified by improved results.

Exercises to encourage the use of following context

Neville and Pugh (1977) found that poor readers appeared to make less use of context following a deletion than good readers in completing cloze tests; this finding was confirmed in this research. Exercises of cloze type with the deletion depending on cues in the following part of the sentence were used to overcome this type of difficulty. Cloze programs in which the readers create and evaluate their own data base have been described by Potter (1984).

Exercises to encourage the processing of complete sentence units

When failing readers lost the theme of the text, the first ability which appeared to be required was the ability to work with all the information from a sentence. Punctuation programs are readily available and can have data bases expanded at a variety of levels. 'Developing Tree', Moy (1984) provides a framework of punctuation within which the meaning and structure of a text can gradually be restored; this program provides for the discussion of all types of reading cues and is a valuable addition to classroom software. Unlike many of the 'drill and practice' programs, it does not isolate a part of the reading process from its proper context nor direct the reader's attention exclusively to cues of one type. The reader is free to decide the type of information which is likely to prove most useful at any point in the process.

Exercises to help establish the nature of connections between sentences

Sentence sequencing as a paper exercise has been widely used in this area. The word processing facility of the microcomputer adds interest and variety to this process and does not involve the teacher in excessive programming or adaptation. Where the computer can be easily used as a substitute for paper exercises, it may increase motivation and effectiveness.

What was the contribution of the computer?

Apart from the visual scanning program, all of the exercises described could be carried out with traditional materials. The remedial programme has now been used with over 30 children giving a mean increase in reading age of 24 months over a six-month period. The main benefits of computer use were in motivating the children and in freeing the teacher.

In deciding whether or not to use the computer and in choosing programs, the following questions seemed important.

(1) Does the program involve whole reading tasks?
(2) Is the program an improvement on traditional material?
(3) Is the type of exercise relevant to the needs of the group of readers?

(4) Does the program provide opportunities for applying the skills developed in meaningful reading?

(5) Does the program encourage the child to express his or her own ideas without fear of rejection?

(6) Is the use of the computer facility an integral part of the program or is it simply an adapted paper and pencil exercise?

The teacher is required to make an informed appraisal of programs in order to choose those which are interesting and appropriate, and must also make an informed appraisal of the needs of the child. A child who presents symptoms of 'difficulty' at word-recognition level may have deeper rooted problems; drill and practice programs which deal with the symptoms may not help to develop effective reading.

If the teacher lacks the knowledge to make these appraisals, inappropriate and ineffective computer programs may become as common as inappropriate and ineffective reading schemes. The tool which is most useful in the classroom is the teacher's expertise. With such expertise, computers may prove valuable aids to reading development; without it, they may simply extend the domain of 'busy work'.

References

BIEMILLER, A. (1970) 'The development of the use of graphic and contextual information as children learn to read'. *Reading Research Quarterly*, 6, pp.75–96.

GRANT, R. and PETERS, T. (1981) 'Classroom diagnosis and remediation for reading difficulties related to binocular instability'. *Remedial Education* (February).

LESLIE, R. and CALFEE, R. C. (1971) 'Visual search through word lists as a function of grade level, reading ability and target repetition', *Perception and Psychophysics*, 10, pp.169–71.

MOY, R. (1984) 'Coming up in the Developing Tree', *Gnosis*, June 1984, pp.16–18.

MULHOLLAND, H. (1984) 'The Interaction with Text of failing and normal readers', unpublished Ph.d. dissertation, The Open university.

NEVILLE, M. and PUGH, A. K. (1977) 'Context in reading and listening: variations in approach to cloze tasks', *Reading Research Quarterly*, 12(1), pp.13–31.

OLIVER & BOYD (1971) Silent Reading Test A, The Schonell Reading Tests, Test R3, Edinburgh O&A.

POTTER, F. (1984) 'Creative language production with the aid of a micro'. Paper presented at U.K.R.A. Conference, Dundee.

List of contributors

Professor Jonathan Anderson
Professor of Education
Flinders University, Australia

Dr Roger Beard
Lecturer
University of Leeds

C. Broderick
Senior Lecturer
North East London Polytechnic

Dr L. John Chapman
Faculty of Education Studies
The Open University

J. M. Ewing
Principal Lecturer in Education and
    Educational Psychology
College of Education, Dundee

Reginald J. Eyre
Senior Lecturer
College of St Paul and St Mary,
    Cheltenham

Rona F. Flippo
Assistant Professor of Reading
University of Wisconsin

Professor Christian Gerhard
George Washington University (D.C.)

Martyn Goff
Director, National Book League
London

Gilbert R. Gredler
Professor of Psychology
University of South Carolina

J. G. Morris
Former H.M.C.I.
Scottish Education Department
Edinburgh

Dr Joyce M. Morris
Educational writer, consultant and
    researcher
London

Helen Mulholland
Principal Teacher Remedial Education
West Calder High School, West Lothian

Anthony J. Obrist
Author
Herne Farm, Dunstable

Dr Frank Potter
Senior Lecturer in Education
Edge Hill College of Education

Peter D. Pumfrey
Senior Lecturer in Education
University of Manchester

C. D. Terrell
College of St Paul and St Mary,
    Cheltenham

Helen C. Tite
Professional Studies Tutor
Nene College, Northampton

Marian J. Tonjes
Professor of Education
Western Washington University

John M. Trushell
Research Assistant
North East London Polytechnic

Steve Walker
Centre for Educational Research and
    Development
Lancaster University

Professor James M. Wallace
Lewis and Clark College, Oregon

David J. Wray
Lecturer in Education
Edge Hill College of Education